The Graduate Student Guidebook

Master Class: Resources for Teaching Mass Communication
Series Editor: Chris Roush

Other Books in the Series:
Master Class: Teaching Advice for Journalism and Mass Communication Instructors by The AEJMC Elected Standing Committee on Teaching and edited by Chris Roush

Testing Tolerance: Addressing Controversy in the Journalism and Mass Communication Classroom by the AEJMC Committee on the Status of Women and edited by Candi Carter Olson and Tracy Everbach

About AEJMC:
The Association for Education in Journalism and Mass Communication (AEJMC) is a nonprofit organization of more than 3,700 educators, students, and practitioners from around the globe. Founded in 1912 by Willard Grosvenor Bleyer, the first president (1912–1913) of the American Association of Teachers of Journalism, as it was then known, AEJMC is the oldest and largest alliance of journalism and mass communication educators and administrators at the college level.

AEJMC's mission is to promote the highest possible standards for journalism and mass communication education, to encourage the widest possible range of communication research, to encourage the implementation of a multicultural society in the classroom and curriculum, and to defend and maintain freedom of communication in an effort to achieve better professional practice, a better informed public, and wider human understanding.

About the Series Editor:
Chris Roush is the Walter E. Hussman Sr. Distinguished Professor in Business Journalism at University of North Carolina-Chapel Hill. In 2010, he was named Journalism Teacher of the Year by the Scripps Howard Foundation and the Association for Education in Journalism and Mass Communication. The judges noted that Roush "has become the expert in business journalism—not just at Chapel Hill, but throughout the country and even in other parts of the world." He has also been named the North Carolina Professor of the Year by the Carnegie Foundation for the Advancement of Teaching and Council for Advancement and Support of Education.

The Graduate Student Guidebook

From Orientation to Tenure Track

The AEJMC Board of Directors
Edited by
Katherine A. Foss

Published in Partnership with the Association for
Education in Journalism and Mass Communication
Elected Standing Committee on Teaching

ROWMAN & LITTLEFIELD
Lanham • Boulder • New York • London

Published in partnership with the Association for Education in Journalism and Mass Communication Elected Standing Committee on Teaching

Published by Rowman & Littlefield
An imprint of The Rowman & Littlefield Publishing Group, Inc.
4501 Forbes Boulevard, Suite 200, Lanham, Maryland 20706
www.rowman.com

6 Tinworth Street, London SE11 5AL, United Kingdom

Copyright © 2020 by Association for Education in Journalism and Mass Communication

All rights reserved. No part of this book may be reproduced in any form or by any electronic or mechanical means, including information storage and retrieval systems, without written permission from the publisher, except by a reviewer who may quote passages in a review.

British Library Cataloguing in Publication Information Available

Library of Congress Cataloging-in-Publication Data

Names: Foss, Katherine A., 1980- editor.
Title: The graduate student guidebook : from orientation to tenure track / edited by Katherine A. Foss.
Description: Lanham, Maryland : Rowman & Littlefield, 2020. | Series: Master class : resources for teaching mass communication | Includes bibliographical references and index.
Identifiers: LCCN 2020010364 (print) | LCCN 2020010365 (ebook) | ISBN 9781538141298 (cloth) | ISBN 9781538141304 (paperback) | ISBN 9781538141311 (epub)
Subjects: LCSH: Universities and colleges—United States—Graduate work—Handbooks, manuals, etc. | Graduate students—United States—Handbooks, manuals, etc.
Classification: LCC LB2371.4 .G725 2020 (print) | LCC LB2371.4 (ebook) | DDC 378.1/55—dc23
LC record available at https://lccn.loc.gov/2020010364
LC ebook record available at https://lccn.loc.gov/2020010365

To those who showed us the way

Contents

Preface ix

Introduction: On Being a Grad Student 1
Katherine A. Foss, Middle Tennessee State University

1 Climbing the Next Rung: Making the Transition to
  Graduate Student 13
  James Stewart, Nicholls State University

2 "This Is Kind of Like Your Superpower": Double-Consciousness,
  Micro-Activism and Other Survival Strategies of Students on
  the Margins 25
  Meredith D. Clark, University of Virginia

3 Graduate Student Decisions 35
  Susan Keith, Rutgers University

4 Getting the Most Out of Your Graduate Assistantship 49
  Amanda Sturgill, Elon University

5 The Mindful Thesis or Dissertation: Finding the Focus to Write 63
  Jan Lauren Boyles, Iowa State University

6 Making Sense of (and Making the Most of) Academic Conferences 75
  Jennifer Greer, University of Kentucky

7 Publishing as a Graduate Student 93
  Denise Sevick Bortree, Penn State University, and Richard D. Waters,
  University of San Francisco

| 8 | Navigating the Job Market: Basic Mechanics and Peculiarities
David D. Perlmutter, Texas Tech University | 113 |
| 9 | The Degree and the Job Are Yours. What's Next? Successfully Transitioning from Student to Professor
Marie Hardin, Penn State University | 129 |

Glossary of Academic Terms 139

About the Contributors 147

Index 151

Preface

At the Board of Directors meetings for the Association of Education in Journalism & Mass Communication (AEJMC), we frequently brainstorm how we can best serve our grad student members. Like most faculty, we want to help, but don't always know how to assist without doing too much and hindering the important voices of those still in school. We were all students once, embracing the newness of the experience, taking our first theory courses, studying for Comps. Although the time since graduation varies, none of us has forgotten the anxiety of the submitted proposal, nor the elation from the first time we were called "Dr."

Yet, we sometimes forget just how much we had to learn, outside of coursework and dissertation prep. I was reminded of these unwritten rules recently. I had received an automated e-mail for a doctoral program, prompting me to submit a recommendation. The problem was, this student had never asked for permission to list me as a reference. While I was initially a bit irked, it dawned on me that he might not be aware of this custom. How do students, even seasoned ones, know about protocol not specifically taught in grad school?

This anthology seeks to fill this gap, offering instruction on many facets of graduate education that one needs to know for success. To identify what topics are particularly bewildering, we turned to the leaders of AEJMC's Graduate Student Interest Group. With their assistance, we created a survey for our student members, which was then revised with input from additional students.

In February–March 2019, we asked participants to identify topics that would have been helpful early on in their higher ed experience. These responses built the table of contents for this book, as advice for assistantships, choosing coursework, thesis/dissertation writing, publishing and other subjects ranked among the most selected. Respondents provided qualitative responses, writing in additional areas in which they wished to have further information. Handling stress, uncertainty, time management and career planning appeared repeatedly throughout the responses.

This survey served as the foundation for this anthology. Written by past and current members of the Board of Directors, we drew on our experiences as former students, faculty, advisors, committee members and AEJMC officers, as well as on the experiences of students and colleagues. Our intention is to steer you through the stages of graduate school, with the hope that you'll sidestep many of the pitfalls that we faced head-on. In reading this, try not to feel stressed and overwhelmed by what seems like a nearly insurmountable climb to graduation. One step at a time.

Introduction

On Being a Grad Student

Katherine A. Foss, Middle Tennessee State University

You've been accepted to graduate school. Congratulations! Now what? The next two to six years are certain to be some of the most difficult, yet rewarding, moments of your life. How do you prepare to set yourself up for success? Well, here's the deal: Part of surviving graduate school is learning the unwritten rules that will help you navigate coursework, advising, comprehensive exams, that daunting dissertation and finally the job market. This anthology will give you a head start so that you arrive at your first class with a sketch of your potential path.

From the beginning of grad school through commencement, you will learn many academic lessons—bodies of theory and methodology, how to synthesize literature, give presentations and conceptualize ideas. What you might not get from your classes, but need to know, is how to succeed at the process. Some of the most challenging takeaways are learned outside of the syllabus or the course objectives. How do you know the best practices of working as a graduate assistant? What are some unique obstacles experienced by international students? Who should be your advisor? Do you choose the big-name scholar in another specialty or the accessible tenure-track faculty that you bonded with in your first class? Once coursework is done and you achieve the coveted ABD (all-but-dissertation) status, you'll start thinking about establishing a foundation for life beyond graduate school. Presenting at an international conference may seem like an impossible feat now, but through your coursework and with the help of your advisor and this book, you'll get to know what to expect and how to make the most of the experience. And at some point, you will be officially "on the market," ready to interview for your first job as a professor (or PhD role in industry).

This book encompasses all the stages of graduate school, with faculty experts sharing their advice and experiences. The first stage, acceptance through starting class, may be the most exciting place of uncertainty. After all, graduate school is a different world from the undergraduate experience or working in the profession. You are about to embark on a journey of exploration, in which you get to spend two to six years reading, thinking, discussing and writing about your interests. And while every course may not be your specialty, you are still within your discipline. Unlike the undergraduate years, you're not taking course after course of gen. ed. No microeconomics for the liberal arts major or intro to badminton to meet an exercise requirement. This is your chance to dig deep into your passion as you figure out who you are and will be as a scholar and teacher. Your new job is to think and learn. Make the most of this time. This introductory chapter will help you prepare to begin school and provide an overview for your grad student adventure.

WHERE TO LIVE

Hopefully, you visited your new city or town before you accepted. If possible, check out housing before you commit to a particular place. Your lodging options will obviously depend on the size, cost of living, and transportation. Acknowledging that this is not a high-income point in your life, you need a quiet, affordable dwelling located somewhere you feel (and will be) safe. Unless you have deep pockets and a real-estate background, I do not recommend buying. Take it from my experience: Nothing is more stressful than trying to sell a house while moving for your first tenure-track job. In fact, I earned tenure before we were finally able to unload our grad school house purchase. This period is just not long enough and too full of uncertainty to offset the costs of home ownership.

So what are some housing choices? Some universities have campus housing for singles, couples or families, which would be convenient, but possibly more expensive. They often have long wait lists so you'll need to apply early. If you are moving by yourself, do you prefer to live alone? How much space do you really need? My first year in the master's program, I lived in a comically small studio apartment, with my dresser in my closet and my bed taking up all of the living space. I did everything there—ate meals, studied, watched TV and slept, of course. It wasn't a good long-term residence, but it did the trick for a little while. You could also share housing or rent a room, if you are open to having roommates. Make sure you thoroughly check out the situation before committing. Ask a person in your new department if there is a listserv or means of communication for you to find an opening. You may want to get to know some people in your program before you live with others in your area. An outside-the-box idea is to look for long-term house-sitting jobs, possibly for a faculty member that is currently on sabbatical. Living in your town for a few months could give you time to figure out the layout and your favorite areas.

For living off-campus, research potential neighborhoods or areas and visit in person, if you can. Which are the closest to campus? If you can walk, bike or skate to class, you'll save so much money and time on the commute. Another option may be to live near a mass transit line. Your university may even offer bus or train pass discounts. Depending on where you live, though, driving might be the only choice. If so, make sure you do your potential commute at the busiest time of the day before you sign a lease. I also recommend exploring the parking options on and near campus and get creative. It would be hard to stomach a $20/day parking fee, but venture far enough out and you may be able to park for free. In my six years of school, I tried out many transportation options. During daytime hours, I preferred parking my car about a mile from my building (the closest free parking), and rollerblading the rest of the way. In the winter, I strapped on plastic bags around my ankles and wore heavy boots, lugging along my shoes and books. For night classes, I parked in a lot with about a ten-minute walk, which was a fraction of the cost of the parking garage.

Regardless of what you think you'd like, try out the commute and parking situation before deciding where to live. The bottom line is that you need a safe place with easy access to campus. You're going to be spending a lot of time there.

PREPPING BEFORE SCHOOL STARTS

If possible, move to your new town with time to adjust. After you've settled in and have done some exploring, start getting ready for your first semester of graduate school. Familiarize yourself online with your new department's faculty, curriculum and other helpful information. You should also figure out your finances before the semester starts. Hopefully you are receiving at least some funding for your graduate coursework. Make sure you know the requirements for maintaining your scholarship, as well as additional benefits. If you will receive health insurance, find out how to enroll and sign up.

Take some time to stroll around campus, visiting the bookstore, library and coffee shop. Contact the graduate coordinator/director of your new program and ask if a current student could meet with you and show you around. I wished I had asked for a tour. I remember awkwardly wandering around my soon-to-be building, feeling like I didn't belong quite yet. I now know that faculty, staff and returning students are excited for the new cohort and are happy to help, even before you've officially begun.

Part of my insecurity in checking out campus stemmed from my anxiety about the unknown. Had I made the right choice? Would grad school be a good fit for me? What if I didn't know the answers or wasn't academically prepared? And, flashbacks from younger years prompted questions about meeting new people, even though I'm a pretty chatty person. Would I have friends? It may seem juvenile, but these feelings are very common and will likely resurface when you eventually graduate and shift into a professional role. Rest assured that most people feel uncertain and that actually starting the program and meeting other students will help you feel more at ease. Two bits of advice to remember at this stage: (1) most newcomers share your feelings and (2) the people you meet in your first days truly want you to succeed.

Many programs offer orientation for new graduate students, especially those who will be working as teaching or research assistants. Make sure to attend these sessions. You'll get an overview of the program and where you typically get set up with a student ID, a parking pass (if you need one), any keys, the code for the copy machine and other logistical obstacles. You'll likely get to see some current students and meet many of your new professors, some of whom will become mentors, advisors, committee members, coauthors and friends.

PLANNING AHEAD

Most programs are fairly structured in the first year or so. If you're lucky, you will get to take a proseminar on graduate school. If not, don't stress. You'll just have to get the lowdown from this book and your new peers. Many students also take introductory theory and methods courses, along with an elective or two. So how should you decide what to take? Look to your advisor (or program director) for recommendations on an appropriate pathway. You want to take interesting classes that will set you up for multiple areas of interest. Check out when the classes meet and think about the logistics of getting there. In my first year, I took an outside-the-department elective located about 30 minutes from the main campus—not a great use of time, particularly because I didn't need the course and I had to battle rush hour.

Sketch out a general plan for your coursework in graduate school, asking about how often courses are offered, what is available online, prerequisites for each course and who typically takes them. You wouldn't want to wind up in an upper-level stats class if you've never taken the intro. Moreover, your courses need to count toward your program. Your coursework should be chosen carefully. It should not be a just a hodgepodge of convenient times and random subjects. You are not just checking requirement boxes but are laying the foundation for your future research agenda.

So what are your goals for your first day? Week? Month? Semester? Year? Degree? It might feel overwhelming to ponder these different steps, especially at the beginning. Yet, you need to lay out where you're going, acknowledging that it is okay for the plan to change. In a particularly helpful grad course I had on teaching, we had to visualize our path to success—literally, by drawing ourselves and the actions toward graduation. I drew myself at a fork in the road at the comprehensive exams, with one path leading me through successful written and oral comps, the dissertation and defense, landing in a tenure-track job. The other route outlined the backup "plan," showing the unsuccessful me working at a Blockbuster video store (dating myself here). This cartoonish drawing hung on a wall in our guest room from that day until we relocated for my job (luckily fulfilling path one). As I surpassed each point on the route of success, I visualized myself as one step closer, never needing to default on the fail-safe life of name tags and plastic movie cases. It wasn't that I doubted my abilities. Rather, including the "failure" route was my humorous way to calm my nerves, serving as a reminder of how far I had come and that I could make it the rest of the way. Each time I glanced at my silly visual aid, I smiled and reminded myself, "one step at a time—and there's always Blockbuster."

Even if the visualization technique isn't your jam, I still recommend outlining rough plans, both in terms of stages and objectives. Working with your advisor, identify the required and elective courses you'd like to take in your graduate study. We'll cover more about what courses in chapter 4. Find out when the courses are offered, how frequently and any prerequisites needed. Ask about any outside-the-department courses you'd like to take so that you'll know of any prep work needed in advance. Outline approximately when you'd like to reach each stage, again consulting with your advisor to make sure your plan is feasible. How long do students typically spend on coursework? At what point do students take comprehensive exams? How many semesters are spent on the proposal before a defense (if there is one)? What is the time lag between proposal defense and thesis defense? Does the graduate school or university require a defense date earlier than the end of the semester? At my current university, to graduate in May, students must defend by March. Finding out this information early can help thwart timing obstacles in the future.

Along with mapping out your stages of progress, consider setting other goals for yourself for the next few years. These objectives may include presenting at your university's scholars' day, traveling to a graduate student workshop or submitting to your professional organization's annual conference. Talk to more experienced students about ways to get involved and expand beyond your coursework. Again, just because you are thinking about these opportunities does not mean you have to do them right away. Before you know it, you will start to feel ready. The plan is the first step in your growth from student to graduate.

STAGES OF GRADUATE SCHOOL

While it might seem like a lifetime away, it's good to have a general sense of what you like to study in your program and the general timeline. The specific courses and number of years will vary by institution, type of degree (master's or PhD), and program. That said, most use a similar path and terminology in the stages of grad school.

1. **Coursework:** You will spend your first years taking a combination of required and elective courses. Most programs have a series of "core" courses that are sequential, covering method, theory and foundational concepts that will prepare you for more in-depth study. You may be able to take courses online and/or in other departments.
2. **Comprehensive Exams (also called "Comps" or "Prelims"):** Once coursework is completed, many programs test students on their overall mastery of the material learned in key areas. These may be open- or closed-book (you might get to choose) and take place over hours or even days. Students often work with advisors and other faculty for a semester or so preparing for these exams. They may consist of just a written portion, just an oral defense or a combination of both. For my PhD program, I had five four-hour written exams (on different subareas) over five days and an oral examination. I could barely remember where I lived at the end of each day. But I studied hard and made it through with coffee, exercise and wonderful guidance. You will too.

3. **Writing the Thesis or Dissertation:** If you are in a doctoral program, passing Comps means that you acquire a special title. You are no longer a PhD student. You are now a *PhD Candidate* or considered *ABD* (all-but-dissertation). Thesis students, your title stays the same, but it's an accomplishment to make it this far nonetheless.

   The next one to three years will largely be an independent endeavor, in which your progress is up to you, aided by your advisor and committee. During this stage, you'll also be attending conferences, publishing and hunting for your first job. Don't worry about all of this right now (but feel free to daydream). One step at a time and good planning will get you there!

STARTING THIS JOURNEY

Much like any new endeavor, the first days can feel really intimidating. Review the syllabi for your courses, while trying not to become overwhelmed. Grad school differs from the undergrad experience as more responsibility is typically put on the students, but with fewer assessments. Many courses will have just one or two research papers and presentations that make up the whole grade. As you look over the reading list, realize that you likely will not read every word in-depth. Your professors will guide you in understanding why each reading was assigned. For example, I assign readings in my qualitative methods course that highlight particular methodologies. Since this is the objective, I expect students to focus primarily on this section, while skimming the remainder of the article.

Sitting in class, you may feel overwhelmed and that are you unique in your feelings. Keep in mind that students come from many different backgrounds and experiences. If you feel lost in the content, know that you are likely not alone. A vocal few may know the answers, but it doesn't mean that everyone does. I remember that in the first week of school, one of my peers (who became a dear friend) spoke up articulately about hegemony. Meanwhile, I was like *"hege-what?"* In other words, it is perfectly okay if you do not immediately know all of the theoretical bodies, concepts and major studies in the field. Do the readings, ask questions and request meetings with your professors if you continue to have confusion.

On the flip side, do not be too laid-back in your approach to graduate school. The unwritten rules you hopefully learned earlier in your education definitely apply here. Do not skip class unless you are truly ill, in which case you should politely e-mail the professor ahead of time.

Plan vacations around the academic calendar. The grad semester is not the time to take a Disney cruise or indulge in your aunt's Palm Springs time-share week. Figure out trips to visit family members outside of your class and assistantship duties. And acknowledge and embrace that you will have work to do at night and on weekends.

Arrive to class early, never late, and ready to discuss the concepts of the week. And, for goodness sake, stay engaged in class, asking quality, relevant questions. I remember one student in my grad days who openly read the (print!) newspaper while the professor was lecturing—as another student in the same class regularly dozed off in front of him. While the instructor did not publicly correct these behaviors, such negative impressions definitely make a difference in grad school success. In addition to staying awake during class, take good notes and refrain from playing on your phone or wasting time online. Expect to stay on campus for some time after class. My grad buddies occasionally remind me of my early grad school gaffe. In my first semester as a master's student, I naively asked if class could be dismissed on time so I could catch the bus. I quickly learned that grad school does not function like *Saved by the Bell* or the "summer vacation" song in *High School Musical*. Class does not necessarily halt when the appropriate end time is reached. Although professors generally finish on time, they decide when it's done, not you.

What I'm getting at is that impressions matter. You never know when a professor might be looking for students to work on a new research project, teach a class or receive a fellowship. And don't forget that you will need faculty members to serve as advisors and committee members, as well as to write letters of recommendations for you. In other words, how you present yourself matters. You want to be known as a "curious, professional student with a strong work ethic," not "Suzie Snoozefest who plays on social media."

You see, the grad student relationship with faculty differs from undergrad. This doesn't mean that you should ditch all work–life balance or that faculty don't have compassion. On the contrary, one of my most beloved professors was very strict in class and with advisees—so strict, in fact, that I remember sweating the day I accidentally left my phone on for fear it would go off (a far cry from my first semester). At the same time, my professor gave everything to her students, providing draft after draft of detailed feedback, pep talks and numerous meetings. She cared so deeply about our success—a trait I've tried to emulate with my own students.

It is also important to have your peers see you as a serious student who is friendly and prepared. The other students that start school with you are your cohort. You will learn, work and grow together. Graduate school is full of group projects and other types of collaboration. Be the person that others seek out. Don't be lazy and idle, but also don't be controlling and arrogant. This cohort is the beginning of your professional network.

How can you set yourself up for success outside of class? Good study habits and a commitment to starting projects early can help ward off last-minute panic. At the same time, as much as you need to devote most of your time and energy to your new endeavor, you also need to have balance. It is not healthy to spend all of your waking hours studying, nor should you regularly sacrifice sleep to make deadlines. Graduate school is a lengthy journey, not a sprint. To do your best, you need to eat real food, get adequate sleep, exercise and take some time for your mental health. I recommend having an activity that takes you emotionally away from coursework and presentations. In the course of grad school, I studied American Sign Language, took trampoline, downhill skiing and gymnastics, and trained (and completed) a sprint triathlon. You will feel better and have more focus if you can take some time for yourself.

GRAD SCHOOL WITH DIFFERENT CIRCUMSTANCES

Every grad student comes to the program with a different perspective, background and set of experiences. I've worked with many international students over the last decade, who have shared some of their unique challenges. Getting used to the food, area and cultural expectations can take some time. If English is not your first language, one student from China advises asking instructors for permission to record lectures, looking for opportunities "to practice your English more" and visiting the campus writing center for extra help. In her experience, "To quickly adapt to the new city, you should actively take part in school or local events and make friends with local people." At the same time, finding fellow international students and faculty or groups on campus can be comforting, as others likely share in your concerns and cultural adjustment.

If you identify as having a disability, planning ahead can help with your grad student experience. In researching programs, check with the campus access center of each institution, asking specific questions about accommodation and resources. Once you are admitted, submit your documentation to the center, working with them, and later on, faculty to establish your needed accommodations for different situations. Don't wait on registering with the disability access center. The process is confidential. And, while most instructors are eager to make accommodations, they can't do so without the proper documentation. Requests are not retroactive. If you delay in registering and find that you aren't doing your best in class, you may not retake tests or turn in late assignments after the accommodation document goes through. The bottom line is to register early and communicate with your professors about what you need to succeed.

Lastly, pregnancy in grad school can pose its own set of circumstances. I won't comment on the timing of pregnancy in school or on the tenure track. What I will say is that once again planning and communication (notice a theme?) will make the process smoother. If possible, check out your health insurance when you or your partner are thinking about or become pregnant. After the news, share it as you feel comfortable with your peers and instructors, particularly with people who may be directly impacted by the timing (i.e., your classroom instructors or those you work for as a teaching or research assistant). You should have an idea about what you'd like to do after delivery—how much time to take off and some contingency plans in case of bedrest or a birth a few weeks early. Grad students are not guaranteed parental leave as with regular employment, at least not at most American institutions. Yet, most instructors will work with you around deadlines. When you return, speak up about your needs, for example, a private space to express and store milk.

AN OVERVIEW OF THIS BOOK

While you can certainly enjoy this book in chronological order, it is designed to be handbook of sorts for your overall grad school experience. In other words, pick it up periodically throughout your grad school experience, focusing on the relevant chapter for your current stage. We are writing this book as current or past Board of Directors members for the Association of Education in Journalism and Mass Communication (AEJMC). While we share this wide discipline, the contributors here draw from an array of institutional and life experiences. We hope this book is useful across fields, spanning from your first days of grad school to the beginning of your career.

In chapter 2, James Stewart addresses the transitional period, from being an undergraduate or a working professional to the graduate student life. Chapter 3 looks at tackling graduate school when you are part of an underrepresented group, as Meredith Clark highlights some of the challenges of entering school as part of a marginalized identity. The following chapter outlines the graduate student decision-making process, in which Susan Keith provides guidance on choosing coursework and advisors, along with offering tips on passing the comprehensive exams. In chapter 5, Amanda Sturgill discusses the ins and outs of working as a graduate assistant, both in teaching and research, helping students get a leg up on their new responsibilities. Then, in chapter 6, Jan Boyles outlines the thesis and dissertation writing process, offering advice on time management, structure, the revision process and handling the proposal and final defenses. The last four chapters shift attention to networking and succeeding on the job market. Jennifer Greer helps readers navigate beyond their own universities, providing insight into maximizing the conference experience, including how to present, network and meet new potential colleagues and collaborators, identify mentors and become more involved with the profession. Since publishing is a crucial step to success, Denise Bortree and Richard Waters address the how-tos of this process, talking about how to publish as a graduate student and beyond, creating the "publication pipeline," shaping a research agenda and becoming an expert on a field of study. In chapter 9, David Perlmutter delves into navigating the job market, addressing each step—attaining letters of recommendation, nailing the conference interview, writing and submitting the application package, landing the campus interview, succeeding on campus and negotiating a solid job offer. Finally, in the conclusion of the book, Marie Hardin addresses your last transition out of graduate school: moving from graduate student into the role of professional. Here Hardin talks about how to overcome imposter syndrome, dress for the part, work with colleagues and other key advice for succeeding at your new role. Congratulations, graduate student! This is the first step in your career!

1

Climbing the Next Rung
Making the Transition to Graduate Student
James Stewart, Nicholls State University

> Just when I think I have learned the way to live, life changes.
> —Hugh Prather[1]

Maybe, as the book says, you did learn everything you really needed to know in kindergarten, but that diploma is probably not going to impress many potential employers. In today's job market, every scrap of sheep's skin is vital to carving out a competitive advantage. With that in mind, you are now attempting the next rung on the educational ladder—graduate school.

As you've no doubt figured out by this point, a big part of navigating the maze of formal education (if you'll forgive the shift in metaphors) is the seemingly constant need to recalibrate your approach to the task. What worked in middle school wouldn't cut it in high school, and college was way different than high school. The academic rigor increased, and everything from social to financial concerns changed along the way. Just when you grew accustomed to the rules, you entered a new game.

Much like the transition from high school student to college undergrad, the advancement to graduate student means taking additional ownership of the learning process. While undergraduates are expected to be more self-motivated and serious about their studies than are high schoolers, most colleges and universities do provide thick safety nets. This is especially true in today's world where there is considerable pressure on institutions to improve retention rates, and the student populations with which they work are comprised of individuals with wildly varying degrees of preparation for the demands of higher education. In your undergrad days, showing up bleary-eyed for class in pajamas or occasionally oversleeping are at least expected (although not exactly appreciated). Like the transition from a part-time job to a career, graduate school is at the next level for behavior, professionalism and opportunities.

Most graduate programs set fairly rigorous standards for admission, and the student population is generally older. Grad students are expected to be more mature and more focused on academic achievement. Evidence of this stance can be seen in the typical requirement that students earn at least a B in graduate courses to proceed. Arriving on time for a graduate class means getting there early (late is *not* an option). If you have to miss class, you are expected to let the professor know as soon as possible and provide an explanation (and there had better be a *very good* reason). The best seats are now at the front of the classroom and you should become *that person* who asks the questions.

Those coming in from the professional world have their own adjustments to make. For those who have been in the job market for a few years, their classmates straight from a bachelor's program may seem *just so damn young*. I mean, really: (for those who don't heed my advice) arriving to class late, making a lame excuse for missed deadlines … that usually doesn't fly with many employers. "Okay Boomer" (or "Gen-Xer") these kids never picked out a movie at Blockbuster or saw a phone attached to a wall. Heck, they may never have set foot in a mall. Deal with it. Sometimes it may be difficult for older, more experienced students to remember they were "that person" a short while back. You may also have different priorities than your fellow classmates. Students who work part- or full-time outside of school, for example, have additional obligations. If you have a partner and/or children, your work–life balance will significantly diverge from single/childless students. In addition, the nature of colleges themselves seems to be changing so rapidly. Mailed final grades changed to Blackboard or other university platform postings; midterm grades became ongoing course averages found on Moodle four-week progress reports on GradesFirst. Readings are often PDFs now. Everything may seem to move at a much faster pace than recalled from undergrad days.

This chapter is intended to help you make the transition from undergraduate or working professional to graduate student. Its information was drawn from interviews with current graduate students, results from an Association for Education in Journalism and Mass Communication (AEJMC) survey of graduate students conducted in 2019, online sources and my own experiences. It may not provide you with specific resolutions to particular problems, but hopefully it will help you think about what the important questions might be.

DO THE RESEARCH

In graduate school, you are responsible for your learning. It's not just about grades but about making the most of the overall experience. Part of increased ownership means asking earlier and more often rather than waiting on someone to track you down (often on multiple platforms) to provide you with important information. I was fairly naïve as a beginning grad student. About the only research I did on the program itself was determining that the school was located near my grandmother's house, so I knew I would have a cheap place to live. I learned just about everything else on the fly, an approach I don't recommend. Today, pursuing a graduate degree is a major financial investment, even with an assistantship or fellowship. Simply getting in doesn't come cheap. "The cost of everything was really overwhelming," one grad student at a large university in the northeast wrote. "Between GRE [Graduate Record Examinations] tests (you pay for the exam itself AND then pay to send out the scores), application costs, transcripts, etc., it was a huge financial burden."

Finding the right school is just the beginning. To maximize your return on investment, you do not, for example, want to be struggling at the start of the semester looking for answers to questions you should have already asked. The first few weeks of a semester are difficult enough; don't add to the burden.[2] Learning university academic policies, personnel, parking rules, social and health programs, or even the campus' physical layout can all be helpful. Throughout this chapter, there will be suggestions on finding resources for answers.

That habit should continue throughout your grad school career. Even in individual classes, you should never be too cool to ask questions of the instructor. Meet frequently with your advisor and/or mentors.

MAKE A PLAN

Accept that you are no longer a member of the 18- to 22-year-old throng meandering across campus. That can be an adjustment in itself. A student at a small southern university said her single biggest adjustment to graduate school was "[o]vercoming an underlying fear that my younger classmates would see me as the weird non-traditional student who asked too many questions that she complained about in her own classes." A graduate education requires many hours of toil outside of class time. Often courses have not *a* textbook but textbook*s*. On top of that, there are usually a significant number of required readings from academic journals. Much of this reading is fairly dense material that can't be absorbed through casual skimming. Piled onto that workload are exam preparation and research for and writing of lengthy papers in pretty much every class. It all adds up to a pretty heavy total. Reflecting on this workload, a professional who returned to a graduate program wrote:

> For ten years, I was focused only on video production, so when I started school, I had to re-focus my attention on reading peer-reviewed journal articles and writing papers every week. It took a couple of months before I was able to fully adjust to working full-time and going to grad school part-time.

ESTABLISH A SCHEDULE

No doubt you have progressed beyond the developmental stage where you have to put considerable effort into choosing between starting to study for that 8 a.m. Monday chemistry exam or one more round of beer pong. You likely have at least close to a full-time job as a graduate student. You may also have a serious relationship. You may have children. And no doubt that you have grown-up bills and have started to worry about things such as insurance deductibles. In short, your life has become much more complicated, and these increasing demands on your time and attention must be considered as you try to find balance between them and the requirements of a graduate program. According to the AEJMC survey, issues related to time management, stress or finances are among the leading concerns of graduate students. A critical part of the maturation process is taking scheduling more seriously, because despite the increased academic expectations, even in grad school, there are still only 24 hours in a day. Developing a formal plan for dividing up that time is therefore a must. The more detailed and extended this plan, the better.

In order for this plan to be effective, it must treat the social and health components of life as seriously as it does work. One student wrote:

> My biggest adjustment [to grad school] was time management. I was very accustomed to enjoying my free time on the weekends. Now my weekends consist of reading, writing, and trying to stay ahead. I still enjoy some free time on the weekends, but I have to schedule it in, or it will not happen.

She added that it is important "to find time to rest and still enjoy life." As a first-year grad student at a large university, it took her a semester to realize that being successful meant focusing on more than her duties as student and grad assistant. "My first semester I was completely absorbed with work, and I didn't allow myself enough time to relax," she wrote. "My second semester I started doing more social things and joined a club that wasn't associated with the school." She added:

> I don't think most graduate students have to be told to work harder. I like to think that if we've come this far, we know how to work hard. However, a lot of us (myself included) aren't great at relaxing and taking breaks. That is also a key part of time management!

Good planning requires time for both studying and the other parts of life that keep you healthy. Sleep is a necessity, not a luxury. Caffeine is not a food group. If you start to feel guilty upon hearing your teachers recount how they made it all the way from their BA graduation ceremony to a submitted dissertation on no more than 15 hours of sleep total, well, let's say hindsight ain't always 20/20 (Do you really think they walked to school *every day* in the snow?).

Chapter 4 will offer more detailed suggestions plotting your path through to degree, but it is worth mentioning here that those little things like looking over the catalog or giving thought to those teachers you might like to study with a semester down the road as you make your plans is time well spent.

DO SOME SCOUTING

Arrive on campus and settle in as soon as possible. There's likely going to be some culture shock when moving to a new area. "I moved from a city to a college town, and it took me an entire semester for it to start feeling like home," one student wrote. "Making friends can be difficult when the work is isolating in nature."

It may not seem all that important, but determining the best routes to a grocery store or which pharmacies are open 24 hours a day or the location of the nearest laundromat can be tremendously helpful. Once again, paying heed to the social aspects of life is as vital to success as is learning degree requirements. Take some to time to find places where you feel comfortable, whether it be a gym, house of worship or cozy coffee shop.

This is even more important for international students: Not only do they have the challenges common to any new graduate student, but there are the supplementary concerns of having to maneuver through the processes of achieving student status under U.S. immigration law, weaving through thicker snarls of university admissions red tape, and acclimating to what might be a vastly different cultural environment.[3]

Arriving early could also afford the chance to meet faculty members in a more relaxed setting than the first day of class. It might be a little difficult to locate them on campus in the gap between summer and fall semesters. Try e-mailing them earlier in the summer or calling to set up an appointment. It's worth the effort because the value of finding a mentor cannot be overestimated.

FIND MENTORS

Throughout this book, we encourage you to find multiple people that can guide you through your program and beyond. When I started grad school, I didn't even know I should be looking for a mentor. By sheer luck, I found three, right at the start. The first was a man who, at the time, was head of the communication school. Fortunately, I had spoken with him several times in the run-up to my first semester. Simply seeing at least one familiar face was tremendously reassuring at the start. The second two initially seemed unlikely choices as mentors for me. At my first meeting with the members of this husband-and-wife team who taught two of the first semester's core courses, they *both* scared the hell out of me. I was quite sure that they saw me as a small-town wannabe who had no business at their fine institution of higher learning. I couldn't have been more wrong. Make no mistake: They expected a great deal out of their students and tolerated little foolishness, but between them, they taught my classmates and me how to prepare for graduate-level exams by synthesizing material from across the program and also how to write scholarly papers. There would be other mentors along the way, but these three helped me start my journey along the right path. Without them, I would likely still be a sports reporter waking up at 5 a.m. to write a recap of last night's 11-year-old all-stars baseball game that ended at midnight the evening before.

You acquire these mentors by talking to faculty members (that's right—by holding an actual conversation during which you find out something about them and they learn about you). The lull between semesters might present the ideal opportunity for those conversations. As one grad student from a large southern university wrote, "Look for someone who has gone before you and blazed the trail you hope to follow. Mentors are there to encourage and guide you."

Mentors can also help with course selection, approaching particular courses or assembling your academic or thesis committees, which some schools require even at the master's level. If an academic committee is going to help you chart your plan of study, finding mentors sooner rather than later is best. I realize that approaching a faculty member as though he or she were a real person may seem a like novel idea, but the relationship between grad students and faculty is different than it typically is for the undergraduate population. This is not to say that graduate faculties exist in some alternate dimension devoid of jerks; they have their share. However, because graduate students are usually more mature and serious about their studies than are undergrads, the social barriers between student and faculty are not as high in grad school as they are at the undergraduate level.

Relationships with mentors do not end at the hooding ceremony. They are a valuable resource throughout you career, giving advice on teaching or research and serving as a critical source of information about job openings or putting in a good word for you when you apply for a post.

APPRECIATE THE VALUE OF "SUPPORT STAFF"

Two other relationships to foster are those with administrative staff and librarians. If you still think that the person working behind the desk in the outer office is a "secretary" whose primary job is to answer the phone, shame on you. You haven't been paying attention. Administrative staff do all the actual work at every organization on the planet. It is very probable that a dean could go missing for months, and no one would notice. If an administrative assistant returns 15 minutes late from lunch, the entire university shuts down. In some cases, the assistants are crucial gatekeepers. They know the important deadlines, where the correct forms are kept, your degree requirements, whom to call about what problem, and where the bodies are buried, so to speak. To this last item, good administrative staffers are incredible fonts of information about the inner workings of an organization and personality quirks. Their advice when considering selection of an academic committee might prove very useful.

Like most people, I didn't spend enough time in the library as an undergraduate. I learned the error of my ways quickly upon entering grad school. In those days, we were using card catalogs and paper indexes to track down material. Once we found the journal article that seemed to fit our needs, we had to hope the library actually had it on site. If the article was fairly contemporary, the odds were usually 60:40 against you—worse than bets on a Vegas roulette wheel. Obviously, modern libraries function much differently, but despite the rumors of print's tragic death, libraries themselves remain amazingly vibrant hubs of information storage and exchange. They do come with their own challenges: While the digital nature of information makes it quicker to access, the sheer volume of material and search platforms has made it somewhat more complicated to find that information.

Librarians have evolved as well. Despite popular perceptions, their main function has never been to shush people (that's just a fun perk). They are archivists and researchers who presumptively have an innate passion for digging out information. In addition to tracking down musty documents, librarians can help you navigate digital databases and locate resources outside of your facilities. For example, is your library a partial or complete repository of federal documents? That's a handy bit of intel if your research area involves congressional testimony. What's the most efficient way to find all *Journalism & Mass Communication Quarterly* articles on the topic of newsroom bias? The librarian knows more effective methods than a Google search. Most likely, they are acquainted with ones that are better than even an "advanced" Google search. Librarians can also connect you with libraries across the country. Through the Interlibrary Loan (ILL) system, you can order books, articles, images, microfilm, microfiche and other documents, which will be delivered to your library within a few days or weeks.

Lastly, librarians can also help you with citation questions for your class papers as they are comfortable with multiple stylebooks. They can also guide you to online resources and other tools that will handle many of the citation protocols for you. Get to know your librarians, treat them with respect, and use them as valuable resources.

REMEMBER YOU ARE NOT ALONE

As with any goal worth achieving, there will be those dark moments when you'll be positive that the degree or certification will always be just beyond your reach. Facing that looming paper deadline with a sick child on your knee or trying to figure out how to get to that exam when the radiator hose on the car is busted and there's not enough money in the bank to fix it, you'll know with absolute certainty that a graduate education was meant for someone else. In that moment, you will be ridiculously wrong.

Several months ago, I had a former student stop by, as she wanted to talk something over. After a number of years in the profession, she had enrolled in a graduate-level certification program at a nearby university. It was within the first few weeks of the semester, and she was upset. The gist of her monologue was: (1) the workload was overwhelming in both volume and nature; (2) the other students had an unfair advantage because they had few responsibilities, boundless energy and degrees from prestigious schools; and (3) she didn't understand much of what she was reading. In short, she felt that she had made a poor decision and that she was never going to make it. In her mind, she was not cut out for graduate school. I told her that I heard in her recitation of anxieties a description of myself as a rookie master's student. At several points, it was a given fact in my mind that I was doomed to flunk out of grad school, forced to scurry home in defeat and shame. I explained that with the exception of those suffering from egomania on an epic scale, everyone who has completed an advanced degree has, on more than one occasion, had those moments of self-doubt, even fear, especially at the start. I was convinced that once she got her footing, graduate-level courses would be a walk in the park. Sure enough, by the end of the semester, she was setting the class curve and had found a mentor. She has now decided to stick around for the master's (I've got my fingers crossed that she goes for the PhD eventually). While there are still plenty of stressful moments, she said, "I look forward to going to class and being challenged. I get excited when my classmates and I have meaningful discussions. I always leave class having more knowledge and understanding than when I arrived."

Getting involved with departmental or graduate student organizations is a good place to start. You will make connections with your fellow students, reminding you that others face many of the same challenges. These groups are another source of information about the program you are in and the broader, postgraduation world. In addition, the social relationships you form will benefit to you while you are in grad school and can create meaningful networking connections in the years to come.

Never be afraid to seek help when you need it. In the movie *The Edge*, Anthony Hopkins' character tells his fellow plane-crash survivors:

> Most people lost in the wilds, they die of shame. [They ask], "What did I do wrong," "How could I have gotten myself into this?" And so they sit there and they die because they didn't do the one thing that would have saved their lives… [t]hinking.[4]

If you are willing to look, there are places to find assistance, where there are people who care deeply about your success.

Checking in with the campus student life office can be an excellent first step. Remember, despite how it may sometimes feel, universities are committed to your achieving your educational goals. They have support operations for both physical and mental health. It is a lot better to get a free flu shot from the university clinic than it is to struggle with the physical and economic expense of actually getting the flu. The mental health centers have special expertise in dealing issues of typical concern among the campus community. There are also offices dedicated to everything from polishing up your writing to career assistance. Some of these operations might be found outside official university offices.

The surrounding communities also likely have places where you can turn for assistance. More often than you expect, there are programs geared toward your specific needs and interests. Veterans' organizations provide support for those in or retired from the military. Religious groups offer services and community functions. There are a wide range of clubs and social groups for populations, including grad, international, minority, LGBT or single-parent students. Locating a community where you feel comfortable and where members have shared experiences can be a tremendous boon.

BELIEVE IN YOURSELF

Reminding yourself why you started the program and accepting that you can complete it are crucial to success. As one student put it quite succinctly, "The most important skills needed to succeed in grad school are motivation and perseverance." It's sort of like running a 5K. For many people, somewhere around mile three, they start to dwell on the fact that it's hot, they're tired and they hurt almost everywhere. The call to stop or at least slow down is so seductive. In order to press on, they think of what they are chasing. For some, it might be setting a personal record. Others are pursuing the pride they will feel from merely finishing (for me, it's the free beer just beyond the finish line. It's a simple equation—the sooner I finish, the shorter the beer line).

It is also vital that you remind yourself that you can do it. "If you weren't capable of doing it, you wouldn't be there," a colleague noted one day when we were discussing the subject of this chapter. Remember: you had to clear a legion of hurdles to just get here. "The opportunity to get an education from a great university is a privilege and blessing, one that is not afforded to everyone," a student pointed out. For example, you earned a bachelor's, and don't minimize having done that. You might be the first in your family with a college degree. About 75 percent of the adult population in this country never completed college, according to the U.S. Bureau of Labor Statistics.[5] But you didn't just finish that degree; you must have performed at a pretty high level. After all, graduate schools require that their students meet both GPA and entrance-exam standards for admission.

CONCLUSION

As I wrote earlier, not a lot people earn graduate degrees. Many never try. Some approach the task haphazardly and stop out when things even appear to head south. The fact that you have made the effort to read this far into this book suggests that you have what it takes to be one of the few. The journey may not be easy, but then few things in life worth having come easily. Overall, the two big things you should take away from this chapter are: (1) there's often help when you need it, so don't be afraid to ask for it, and (2) have confidence in yourself when your world looks terrifying, which every grad student's does on occasion.

NOTES

[1] Hugh Prather, *Notes to Myself: My Struggle to Become a Person* (New York: Bantham Books, 2009), 41.

[2] CollegeXPress, "Top 10 Tips for International Graduate Students," accessed October 28, 2019, https://www.collegexpress.com/interests/international-students/articles/find-right-us-university-you/top-10-tips-international-graduate-students/.

[3] CollegeXPress, "Top 10 Tips for International Graduate Students."

[4] swordfishblackfox, "The One Thing—Motivational—Anthony Hopkins," February 10, 2012, video, accessed January 28, 2020, https://www.youtube.com/watch?v=9PRZW0C6-ms.

[5] "Profile of the Labor Force by Educational Attainment," accessed October 30, 2019, https://www.bls.gov/spotlight/2017/educational-attainment-of-the-labor-force/pdf.

2

"This Is Kind of Like Your Superpower"

Double-Consciousness, Micro-Activism and Other Survival Strategies of Students on the Margins

Meredith D. Clark, University of Virginia

I think about being a Black woman a lot. I think about *my being* as a Black woman even more. To be honest, I think about it every day.

Not so much while I'm in my home, but how the world sees me, when I step just outside my door. Like the faint fingerprints of the Black enslaved laborers in the bricks of buildings I pass along the seven-minute walk between the student apartment building where I live, and the office where I work, the enduring evidence of how power defines identity. In turn, how I move through and am viewed in this world is something I can never un-see, and thus, can never afford to forget.

While AEJMC and its members have engaged in good-faith efforts to draw people from underrepresented backgrounds into journalism and mass communication, the discipline and its institutions are still characterized by markers of white, male, heterosexual norms—what most call "the dominant culture." For many of us, navigating this terrain requires a secondary skill set. And to paraphrase (as a friend often quips) "what thus saith the Lorde," my silence about this knowledge has not saved me. Yours will not save you. So let's talk in frank terms about what it means to engage in self-care as an act of political warfare in academic worlds where we, people who are somehow *different*, are navigating the path from student to scholar.

For the purpose of this chapter, I trust that a brief reflection on four dimensions of the self—personal, professional, scholarly and communal—will offer common ground and practical insights that apply to a wide swath of folks from underrepresented backgrounds. Admittedly, some of this advice already falls short, as it collapses difference into a single category rather than the considering the particulars of why a chapter like this one is necessary in such a volume.

SELF-CARE IS NON-NEGOTIABLE

In our always-on, always connected world, mantras of self-care are becoming normalized, even as they are mocked by people who see them as self-indulgent. They are not, particularly for people from underrepresented groups. When being who you are requires navigating norms that position your existence as deviant in some way, shape or form, both mind and body require extra care and attention.

Overwork, with its ableist and classist assumptions of what it means to be *seen as* constantly engaged in knowledge development, production and transfer, may be the unspoken ethos of academia, but it does not have to be yours.[1] Graduate students are often advised to be seen working in the office or feel pressured to perform productivity in ways that others before them have done. Decide what your boundaries will be, what measure is "enough," and how you will care for yourself when you've had to push past your limits. Recognize that each of these indicators may change with the rhythms of the academic year, the phase of your program, and the external demands of your life away from campus.

For Black women, this sort of self-care is essential to protecting against "weathering," the often-invisible physiological and psychological stressors that allow us to *look* like we're not hurting, while shaving years off our vitality.[2] Among people on the margins, even everyday occurrences can be characterized by invisible challenges. For instance, one gender non-conforming graduate student I spoke to about this chapter mentioned the fatigue of having to repeatedly remind professors and students alike of their use of they/them pronouns. This sort of internal work is the terrain of the "queerly ordinary"—the micro-activism of personal maintenance that trans folks do to simply make it from day to day.[3] No matter what makes each of us different as people from underrepresented backgrounds, we all have specific compelling reasons to find out what works for us, and to operate from that knowledge as part of our approach to academic life.

When Dr. Felicia Harris, assistant professor at the University of Houston-Downtown, first shifted away from her initial aims of running a hyper-local news site in her hometown and enrolled in her PhD program, she had a particularly compelling external motivator for navigating personal-professional boundaries: her then 4-year-old son, Omari.

I feel like when people found out (I was a single parent) they thought it was a horrible thing that happened to me. But I don't how people did it *without* kids. Not only did he give me a structure, he gave me a reason. This is kind of like your superpower. It allows you to do things that people have not considered. I ran my life like an 8-5 job. My days would start 6:30 or 7. [I'd] wake him up, get him dressed, work out, come home, shower, go down to my desk. Work from 9 to 1. Class from 1 to 3 or 4.

I had him in after-school care to give him socialization, and to give me time to work. Pick him up, shut the world out from 6 to 8:30, and he had a strict bedtime at 8:30. And I'd work from 9 to 1 a.m. It was hard as hell, but I was the first one to defend in my cohort. Because I wasn't doing what everyone else was doing. I ran a tight ship. I was so organized that I have struggled to find balance without being that rigid.[4]

Before you begin your graduate program, or perhaps, as soon as you read this, take some time to reflect on who you are, and what you need to be at your best. How much rest do you require? What kind of food nourishes you and provides you with the most energy? What kind of physical activity makes you feel like your body is running optimally? How can you structure your day to be your best self? Not your "ideal" self, but the person who is capable of showing up prepared to contribute in ways that make sense for the lifestyle you want to lead as a graduate student, and eventually, as a professor or industry professional.

MAPPING YOUR PROFESSIONAL MENTORING NETWORK

Before my first semester in the PhD program, one of my external mentors, Natalie Tindall (Lamar University), warned that "graduate school will change you." And it does—in some profound, often indescribable ways. As a professional, being consistent with your values and integrity, even when experience shifts your perspective, is one way to maintain a sense of stability. Connecting with mentors who have mastered the professional aspects of living a life of double-consciousness[5] in the academy is another.

Kerry Anne Rockquemore, founder of the National Center for Faculty Development and Diversity, suggests the development of a network of mentors.[6] Business author Carla Harris also touches on this concept—distinguishing between a mentor, an advocate and a sponsor.[7]

Marcos, a professor who asked to tell his experience with mentoring anonymously, also advocates that students from underrepresented groups consider having both formal and informal mentors. "I had a very uncomfortable experience where a senior faculty member came up to me and told me that the subject of my dissertation was too marginal, that it was a byproduct of my identity. And that it was too narrow of a topic to get a job," he said.

I had to teach professors of mine and the IRB what trans was, and why trans was different from gay. I think a lot of minority grad students and professors have to do is this work of translation of translating what you're doing in ways that those folks who are not familiar with it can understand. I found it frustrating, but it also helped me; it helped me think about "how do you talk about this specific thing in a way that a larger audience can appreciate?"

But it was also discouraging; a little exhausting. But this is where the role of mentoring comes in: I had an official mentor and an unofficial mentor. When I came to my official mentor—who was a woman of color—she was supportive. And I had an unofficial mentor who would read my stuff every now and then. And she was a feminist researcher, so she totally got it. For me, realizing that these are two really successful, productive, well-known scholars in their field, who say "yes, your project is important and worthy, and yes, you are studying a marginal group, but yes, we will support you," was everything.[8]

I encourage you to build your mentoring networking in three directions: up, consisting of scholars and professionals whose career objectives inspire your own; across, consisting of colleagues and peers whose experience is within a few years of your own; and down, lifting others with you as you climb. You should have at least three people in the first category, two in the second, and one in the third. These numbers will shift, grow and change as your career progresses, but they will give you the opportunity to develop a mentor, a sponsor and an advocate; a reader and/or a collaborator, and to serve as a champion for at least one other person. Some of the most successful early career professionals in our field found their collaborators early, either in their own programs or via networking at conferences and subject-specific meetings, and have developed both co-mentoring and coauthoring relationships that allow both to get feedback on their work and publish with frequency.

SURVIVING ON STIPENDS

Financial management is also critical at this time. We come from a number of different economic backgrounds. Like me, you may have been a working professional before you entered graduate school, choosing to take a major pay cut while pursuing a terminal degree. Or your assistantship may be the first consistent salary you've experienced. For many of us, there is no safety net of family or robust savings to support us as we pursue graduate education. Academia assumes a certain degree of wealth. For instance, many universities operate on a fiscal schedule that issues the first disbursements of the academic year as late as October 1. If you have quit your job in July or just switched cities, it may be some time before you receive your first paycheck. Students are also often expected to pay out of pocket for conferences and meetings, and reimbursements can take months to be processed. One strategy is to calculate the dollar amount you need to live for one month to six weeks, and try to have that available. There is no magic formula. Some of us come to it by savings, some by loans, some by credit cards, many by a combination of the three. Think of the long-term implications of each, and plan accordingly.

Know your university's travel policies before you plan to submit for conferences and other meetings. There's often a gulf between the reality of transportation, lodging and meal costs, and the federal per diem guidelines that your university uses for reimbursement. In my experience, doing the administrative work related to finances is one of the most maddening tasks you'll encounter in your early career years. If possible, you may want to secure a credit card expressly for school-related travel use to separate these expenses out. I encourage you to pack a large plastic or manila envelope to keep all of your receipts and documents (get printouts of hotel receipts before you check out; e-mails get lost, zapped etc.). Take 30 seconds to snap a picture of *every* receipt you generate in the moment it touches your hand, from the time you leave home to the time you return. As far as reimbursements go, those receipts are the proxy for your cash.

Finally, find out what professional services and professional development opportunities are available to you. Rockquemore's center, for instance, offers on-campus workshops, webinars and other resources for professional development. Karen Kelsky's website and column, The Professor Is In, has addressed a number of questions common to graduate students, covering everything from approaching a potential advisor to negotiating job offers. And on campus, everything from libraries with dedicated personnel who can assist with systematic literature reviews and deliver books, to graduate student-specific meetings that allow you to workshop your work in the company of a sympathetic audience, to university-wide travel grants that will support your conference attendance or field research, there are a number of support systems that can be marshaled to assist you during these years.

PURSUING THE LIFE OF A SCHOLAR

Developing as a scholar requires two basic intrinsic qualities: a strategic outlook and a tenacious spirit. That's it. The rest—subject-matter knowledge, time and resource management, academic prose, presentation skills, effective teaching—is learned, as chapters in this volume illustrate. Your central objective is to earn your degree with your health and sanity intact, and to use it in the career that suits your interest. Most of the advice in this book is prepared with the assumption that you want to be a career academic, focusing on research and teaching. Alternative academic (alt-ac) careers are becoming more common as the rate of degree earners outpaces the number of available jobs in our field, yet there is still some stigma in programs about pursuing the PhD, in particular, without the intention to use it to become a professor. Either way, you will need to approach your education as a long game—one where you have significant power to shape the rules.

As an emerging scholar, you are becoming an expert in one thing. Most graduate programs are not designed to promote exploration. Unlike undergrad, the assumption is that you will arrive with a clear understanding of what you want to study, and who you want to study it with (your faculty/dissertation advisor), and to some extent, how you want to study it. These insights should drive what program you choose to enter, and who you select as a formal academic mentor. Beyond that, it's up to you to make out a clear path to your degree.

Begin with the end in mind, as Stephen Covey has advised.[9] Take some time at the beginning of each term to ask yourself reflexive questions about how the courses you're taking and research you're doing will inform your dissertation and the procedural hurdles you must clear to get to it. Early on, I was advised to use each class to somehow inform my dissertation. My methods courses became sites for piloting the approaches I'd use in my dissertation research; my theory courses were for deep reading on the frameworks specific to my questions. The reading list for my comprehensive exams was culled from a combination of course syllabi, works I found and cited in my own papers, and new, related publications from the journals where I wanted to one day publish. Subject-matter courses helped me advance my knowledge of the subfields connected in my work. For instance, it was my anthropology class on ethnography in Black communities that served as the creative grounds for my digital ethnography of Black communities on *Twitter*—the subject of my dissertation. Feedback on a term paper became comments on an unofficial "revise and resubmit," moving it from a course requirement to a conference paper, with the aim of publishing it as a peer-reviewed journal article.

I learned to approach the learning process this way only through the connection of scholars of color who passed down otherwise unspoken insights to help me navigate the new academic terrain. Unlike our earlier academic pursuits, graduate education expects that we will continually build on the things that we learn and do, ultimately producing tangible outcomes in the form of presentations and papers. The grades, while critical, are not the key objective. Producing rigorous scholarship is.

GET CONNECTED WITH COMMUNITY

In *Sisters of the Yam: Black Women and Self-Recovery*, bell hooks details the importance of community in maintaining your sense of self in academia.[10] hooks acknowledges the reality of pursuing higher education—that the choices we make often lead us far from home and any semblance of familiarity, and thus encourages us to develop community wherever we find ourselves.

Entering her graduate program, Felicia Harris said, marked the moment "when I learned to be intentional about building a community of people who I could trust. ... I sought out people who liked kids and had kid energy. They would take Omari to the zoo, and I would be able to go to the library for like three hours. The community of people was pivotal," she said.

During my years at UNC-Chapel Hill, finding community meant choosing to live in Durham, the more affordable, more racially and culturally diverse city 15 minutes away from campus; finding a church home with traditions that provided comfort; and joining the Black Graduate and Professional Student Association. If you've moved to a new city and can spare a few hours (I worked my last day one Friday and began school 600+ miles away the following Tuesday), take time to learn about its history and how that history has shaped the experiences of people like you. Local libraries and historical associations often offer free programming of this nature. Set aside some time each month—but preferably every week—to experience your community *outside* of the university, where you can be reminded of life outside of the academy. You will need the reality check every now and again.

I encourage you to find some of the spaces that will affirm you both off and on campus, but particularly in the community where you will live. These spaces are havens when you're working through some of the particulars, like editing your papers, getting some reading done, or when you just need to step away from student life for a moment. Where can you study, meet with friends, have a private and candid conversation, or just sit in silence to read, get work done and/or decompress?

Fortunately, the modern affordances of social media offer graduate students unparalleled connectivity with other students and potential mentors. On *Twitter*, hashtags like #TrynaGrad, #CiteASista and #BlackGradLife are used to promote transparency and discussion about individual experiences. Following them, or at least checking in with them on a weekly basis, may help you discover resources and gain valuable perspective on your own experience. Each week, these hashtags help me to see what graduate students across the country are experiencing in their program, and what I can do to help.

They're also useful for connecting to find resources (including access to articles in journals beyond your university library's system), and developing ideas about the ways your work fits into larger social worlds.

Podcasts, too, are useful for developing community beyond the borders of your institution. Imagine Otherwise is a podcast hosted by Cathy Hannabach that interviews scholars working at the intersections of academia and social justice to engage in candid conversation about process, discovery and possibility. It's a useful touchstone for thinking about our work outside of the confines of courses, papers, conferences and presentations. "Andazuling It!", by two queer Latinx folx, has a strong West Coast vibe as part of its narrative theme; while "Identity Politics," by Ikhlas Saleem and Makkah Ali, explores identity along intersecting lines of race, gender, class and religion. For professional development, "Research in Action," by Katie Linder, and "Teaching in Higher Ed," by Bonni Stachowiak, are two of my favorites for learning more about how people address their work.

As you read this volume, know that its contributors have created it with the hope that you will find community within AEJMC, as many of us did. While the information presented in it is designed to address the practical concerns of graduate education—ones that are common to us all—we recognize that race, gender, class, sexual orientation, gender expression, nationality, religion and additional markers of difference often have an indelible influence on even the most basic of processes. Be encouraged. You are in your program because scholars who have been where you are now recognize that you have perspective that our field needs—in the classroom, in the literature, in the world.

NOTES

[1] Nicole Brown & Jennifer Leigh, "Ableism in Academia: Where Are the Disabled and Ill Academics?," *Disability & Society*, 33, no. 6 (2018): 985–989, DOI: 10.1080/09687599.2018.1455627.

[2] Arline T. Geronimus, "The Weathering Hypothesis and the Health of African-American Women and Infants: Evidence and Speculations," *Ethnicity & Disease*, 2, no. 3 (1992): 207–221.

[3] Andre Cavalcante, *Struggling for Ordinary: Media and Transgender Belonging in Everyday Life* (New York: New York University Press, 2018), 177.

[4] Dr. Felicia Harris (assistant professor) in phone call with the author, January 2020.

[5] William Edward Burghardt Du Bois, *The Souls of Black Folk: Essays and Sketches* (Chicago: A.C. McClurg, 1903), 7.

[6] Kerry Ann Rockquemore & Tracey Laszloffy, *The Black Academic's Guide to Winning Tenure Without Losing Your Soul* (Boulder, CO: Lynne Rienner Publishers, 2008).

[7] Carla Harris, *Expect to Win: 10 Proven Strategies for Thriving in the Workplace* (New York: Hudson Street Press, 2009), 101–127.
[8] Marcos (tenure-track professor) in interview with the author, January 2020.
[9] Stephen R. Covey, *The Seven Habits of Highly Effective People* (New York: Free Press, 1989), 95–144.
[10] bell hooks, *Sisters of the Yam: Black Women and Self-Recovery* (New York: Routledge, 1993), 113–124.

3

Graduate Student Decisions

Susan Keith, Rutgers University

Graduate student life is a series of choices and requirements. You decide to go to school. You choose your program. You select a path of study. You pick courses. You select an advisor. At the same time, there are requirements. You must attend classes, write papers, take comprehensive or qualifying exams and complete some sort of culminating work: a project, a thesis or a dissertation. If you're just beginning the grad school journey, navigating these choices and requirements can feel overwhelming. This chapter aims to help. It offers some reflections on the major milestones of graduate school, drawing on my experiences teaching master's students, and serving as the advisor or interim advisor for 21 PhD students. The chapter also reflects my own experience and occasional befuddlement in graduate programs, as someone who came to academia after a career in journalism.

CHOOSING A PATH OF STUDY

Two key graduate school choices—your area of study and your advisor—are intertwined, and usually are part of the decision about which programs you considered. Once you have been admitted and start to narrow your focus, you might want to ask yourself two questions:

- What subfield within my discipline fascinates me?
- What area of study will help me get a job, either in academia or industry?

Your area of study should be one you will be passionate about for the long run. Master's programs typically last 1–2 years and PhD programs 3–6 years or longer! (Illnesses, babies, taking care of aging relatives, and other significant disruptions can slow student progress.) If you're studying a topic you only *sort of* like, you'll be sick of it by the time you complete a project, thesis, or dissertation.

Whatever your passion, it's also important to think practically about what the focus of your graduate studies will mean for return on investment in time and tuition dollars (*if* you pay them; some master's programs and most doctoral programs remit tuition as part of graduate assistantships). The third decade of the 21st century probably wouldn't be a great time, for example, to start a professional skills-based master's degree focused on print newspaper page design. But it might be a good time for a professional master's courses in online user experience design or computational journalism.

PhD students planning to look for faculty positions also have to consider their specialties carefully. As this chapter was being written, for example, media and communication units around the United States were eager to hire PhD graduates in strategic communication (public relations and advertising), as well as job candidates whose vitae combined work experience in and theoretical understanding of digital media. In-demand fields change over time, though, so it's a good idea to examine academic job advertisements in the *Chronicle of Higher Education*, on InsideHigherEd.com, and on the websites, e-mail lists, and social media of AEJMC and other academic organizations.

Those ads, of course, can pinpoint only current needs, not where disciplines are headed. To protect yourself, it's a good idea to ground your work not in a medium or platform but in broader concepts about the field and how they are used. For example, even though you might want to examine in your studies how people use a particular social media platform, such as *Twitter*, to engage with political action, you should think about the core of your research as being media and political engagement, not *Twitter*. Framing your work conceptually, for yourself and others, helps you avoid the "I study MySpace" problem, referring to the decline of what was the largest social networking site from 2005 to 2008. *MySpace* faded in popularity after the launch of *Facebook* and lost more than a decade of data in 2019.[1] Focusing too narrowly on a particular technology, such as on a specific site, risks making your work look out of date quickly.

SELECTING AN ADVISOR

What you study, of course, is usually closely related to who guides the process. Most master's and PhD programs require each student to have an advisor, a faculty member who shepherds the student's academic work and chairs the committee that reviews the student's final master's thesis or project or doctoral dissertation. You should think about who that advisor might be as you apply to graduate schools—"Would you take a job for a minimum of four years without knowing who your boss would be?" asks Robert L. Peters, author of *Getting What You Came For: The Smart Students Guide to Earning a Master's or PhD*.[2] At the same time, the real work of securing an advisor, in U.S. graduate programs, generally comes once you arrive on campus.

Graduate programs vary on how advisors and advisees are paired. In some programs, like the doctoral program where I earned my PhD, students were assigned an advisor upon admission, paired with the faculty member who seems to offer the best scholarly fit. In other programs, like the media studies area of the interdisciplinary PhD program I teach in, all students in a cohort are paired with an interim advisor and expected to choose a permanent advisor later. There are advantages and disadvantages to both systems. The assigned-advisor-upon-arrival approach gives students an immediate anchor in a sometimes confusing new situation. But students whose interests change can find it stressful to "break up with" that assigned advisor. The wait-to-choose-a-permanent-advisor approach lets students avoid changing advisors, but it can leave them without advice from a particular subfield perspective about the choices they make early in their program, such has choosing courses.

The perfect advisor would be an expert on the media objects or communication practices that you want to study, the methods you plan to employ and the theories that will be important for your work. In addition, the perfect advisor would share your temperament and communication style and have these attributes that PhD students in one survey-based study identified:

- Accessibility
- Helpfulness in making clear informal program rules
- Ability to socialize students to the academy and field
- An attitude of caring about you as a whole person[3]

There are, however, no perfect advisors! Many, if not most, graduate students have to make at least one compromise as they choose a project, thesis or dissertation supervisor, perhaps in topic area, theoretical framework or method. If you want to study how audiences use podcasts for entertainment, you might find that no one on the faculty of your program has expertise in that precise area. There may, however, be professors with knowledge in the related areas of audience studies, radio studies or entertainment studies.

Some divergence between the work of advisor and advisee can enrich both participants. I had expected before I entered my PhD program that I would work with a scholar who used social science approaches in thinking about media ethics. I learned when I arrived at the university, however, that he was moving into phased retirement and that I had been assigned to a different faculty member. Her primary area, media law, became my secondary area during my graduate studies; her secondary area, media ethics, was my primary focus. Not all advisor/advisee matches will work, of course. A faculty member who studied media depictions of race and ethnicity using quantitative content analysis and didn't believe that qualitative approaches constituted "real" research would not be a good advisor for a PhD student who wanted to study race and ethnicity in the media using Foucauldian discourse analysis and postcolonial theory.

Two factors that I would argue are not negotiable in an advisor are respect for your work, including the methods you use, and availability. My advisor, Dr. Ruth Walden, and I had similar temperaments and work ethics, and she was amazingly willing—as a full professor—to learn new things and support me in doing the dissertation I wanted to do, even when it forced her to stretch. When I decided to survey journalists as part of my dissertation work, requiring university institutional review board (IRB) approval, she devoted hours to taking the required human subjects training so that she could sign my IRB research proposal. She also remained available to work with me, even as she took on new advisees and I moved more than 2,000 miles away before finishing my dissertation. On one occasion when I flew back to meet with her, we spent hours poring over my survey questionnaire at her dining room table on a Saturday afternoon—a truly exceptional act of honoring my research.

You should be aware, however, that the structures of academia can affect advisor availability. If you might need to consult with an advisor during the summer, you should ask whether a potential advisor is available then. Faculty members on nine- or ten-month contracts generally aren't paid for working in the summer, and some, quite reasonably, protect precious research, recuperative or family time. You should also inquire about whether your potential advisor will be away from the university on a sabbatical or another type of leave during key parts of your work and, if so, how that would affect your completion.

The number of advisees a professor has also can affect availability. "Star" faculty members may attract many advisees, especially if they are successful in helping students work on interesting projects, craft conference papers, publish work, complete on time or find jobs. At least one study indicates, however, that advisor prominence is less a factor in doctoral graduate early-career scholarly production than where a student was trained, with students strong enough to be attractive to top PhD programs doing better than students in lower-rated programs, whoever their advisors were.[4] The best strategy may be to have the star as a committee member with a more "junior" faculty member, who has a lot of time to devote to a PhD student, as the chair.

Finally, if you are considering asking an assistant professor to be your advisor, find out where that faculty member is in the timeline toward tenure and consider making sure that at least one other committee member has the expertise to advise your work. Some academic units have wisely put policies in place that keep assistant professors from advising—at least without a co-advisor—until they have passed a preliminary milestone, such as a third-year or fourth-year review. If your program doesn't have such a policy, you should take steps to ensure that you're not left with no one to advise you if there is an unfavorable tenure decision.

Graduate students sometimes have difficulty approaching their identified potential advisors, fearing that they will turn them down. Over the years I have found myself in a number of conversations with doctoral students who wanted me to guess their chances of getting some *other* faculty member to advise their dissertation—a situation that reminded me of the eternal seventh-grade lunchroom question "Do you think she/he likes me?" I've sometimes been in the awkward position of knowing that a graduate student planned to ask one of my colleagues to advise weeks before the student found the courage, and the moment, to do so.

Your advising request shouldn't come as a surprise to the faculty member you approach. If you have been an enthusiastic participant in a professor's course, read and asked questions about the professor's research, and attended talks or programs organized by the professor, the faculty member will probably expect you to ask about advising. Sometimes, however, you may need to approach a professor whom you haven't taken a course with or don't know well. In that case, you might want to start with an e-mail something like this:

> Dear Professor,
> I'm starting to think about putting together the committee to advise my (project/thesis/dissertation), and I would like to schedule an appointment to talk with you about my ideas for the work. I read your (book/article/book chapter) about X, and I am interested in the topics you wrote about/theory or method you used. I have attached a paper/essay/class assignment/summary related to my project, along with a copy of my vita/resume. Would you have a chance to meet soon?
> Thank you,
> Your name

Such a note gives the faculty member the chance to assess your writing and motivation and to understand how much work advising you might require.

Once you have an advisor, what then? I think it's a good idea to discuss expectations for the arrangement. Will you meet regularly? Does your advisor collaborate with students? Or does the advisor operate in a model of encouraging you to create your own work, which the advisor will read in drafts? What are the expectations for key timeline moments, such as completing coursework, taking comprehensive or qualifying exams, or turning in a thesis or dissertation proposal? I have taken different approaches with different students, meeting frequently in person with advisees who were on campus taking or teaching courses, and meeting less frequently and corresponding via e-mail, text, phone and Skype with students who live further away or prefer to work more independently. One of my advisees, knowing I often work late at night (a habit from my pre-academic years as a newspaper copy editor), frequently sent me complex questions about legal decisions by e-mail at midnight, suspecting (rightly) that I would answer them before he got up in the morning. Some advisors, however, prefer that all advisees follow more structured schedules of meeting weekly or monthly.

Despite asking all the right questions up front, you may find that you need to change advisors. Your advisor may retire, become ill or die, fail to earn tenure or move to another university. You may decide to study in a different area or conclude that you and your advisor are not temperamentally suited to working together. If your advisor remains a part of your program, you should proceed with sensitivity. This person may have advocated for you to be admitted, over other qualified applicants; counted on your expertise in a research project; or expected that the work of advising you would count toward tenure and/or promotion. Approach your desire to change straightforwardly and in a face-to-face meeting; you shouldn't end an advising relationship by e-mail. You don't want your current advisor to find out that you're thinking of making a change by hearing about it from another faculty member. You shouldn't tell your advisor obliquely, as one of my former advisees did, by listing the faculty members who would be on his qualifying exam committee and leaving me off the list!

In the academy, as in other workplaces, there are people who are not good at some aspects of their jobs. As periodic articles in the mainstream and higher education press chronicle, a few faculty members are overly critical, unresponsive or sarcastic in dealing with advisees.[5] They may get away with this behavior because in their work as advisors, as one anonymous writer put it, they "don't appear to be accountable to anyone."[6] If you find yourself with an advisor like this, changing as soon as possible is probably the best option. You should also share your experience, but be careful of taking it only to the newest assistant professors. They may be the most sympathetic, because their graduate school experiences were the most recent, but they also have the least power in a unit, and they may not be in a position to openly criticize your more senior faculty advisor, who will be voting on their tenure case. Speaking with a graduate director, department chair or academic dean is a better strategy.

SELECTING AND SUCCEEDING IN COURSEWORK

A good advisor can help you make wise choices about graduate coursework, a required feature of master's and doctoral programs in the United States. (Programs in the United Kingdom and many other countries traditionally have been based primarily on a research apprenticeship model, rather than coursework.[7]) Most U.S. programs at both the master's and doctoral levels have some required courses, often covering theories and methods, as well as electives based around faculty members' research interests.

Not every elective course will be offered every semester. So it's important to strategize about which courses will help you produce the project, thesis or dissertation you think you want to create. You might sit down with the list of elective courses from your program, circle those that seem related to your scholarship and then rank them by which seem most crucial. Will your thesis or dissertation be stronger if you take a course in media studies theory? Do you plan to use a method that will be strengthened by that elective methods course in online ethnography? Once you have narrowed a list of electives to a handful, talk to your advisor or graduate director about which are likely to be offered when.

You may also want to look for elective courses from outside your program. Many graduate programs allow, if not require, students to take electives in other departments. While studying for a master's degree in journalism studies, I took an elective course in modern art history that produced my first AEJMC Southeast Colloquium paper and inspired my now decades-old interest in mid-20th-century abstract art. You may also find that you can earn a graduate certificate in another unit that will make you more interesting to potential academic employers. For example, the Department of Women's, Gender, and Sexuality Studies at Rutgers University, where I teach, offers a three-course graduate certificate that some School of Communication and Information PhD students earn because they are interested in representations of diversity in the media. Your university may also allow you to take courses beyond your campus. When I was a doctoral student at the University of North Carolina at Chapel Hill, I took a mind-blowingly wonderful 20th-century philosophy course at Duke University. Students in my PhD program at Rutgers can take courses at universities in New York and Pennsylvania as well as New Jersey.

Once coursework begins, some graduate students have trouble keeping up with a reading load that may be very different from what they encountered in undergraduate programs, where texts "often construct knowledge as uncontestable."[8] Graduate students, especially those in PhD programs, are expected not merely to understand the ideas in readings, but to compare and critique them, placing their own ideas into conversation with the ideas they have encountered in readings. In doing so, students gain vital preparation for becoming knowledge-constructors themselves. This work, however, is not always easy. Academic writing often deals with complex concepts, and even the most insightful authors often could use more editing than they get. So parsing the meanings of key texts can be a challenge. In addition, because academic research is accretive, with new scholarship building on (or beside, or around) work that came before, there can be a sense that you're always entering in the middle of things. You have to try to understand current thinking about a concept, theory or method as well as how that reasoning developed and in what contexts. Ideally, you also should think about where the concept, theory or method could be taken in the future.

Because there is rarely enough time to read everything in a subfield, academics have developed triage strategies. Some scholars suggest reading the reference list of a work first, to develop a sense of where it fits with existing literature. Entrepreneur-turned-academic Kevin P. Taylor—as of this writing a PhD student and senior instructor in business at DePaul University—suggests reading in layers. He first approaches a work by reading its title, abstract and/or cover material, and table of contents, along with any relevant reviews. If that surface reading suggests the material is relevant, he reads introductions and conclusions, skims method and analysis sections, and figures and tables.[9] It is in layer-three reading that Taylor does the heavy lifting of graduate school scholarship, questioning everything: "assumptions, methods, sample, validity, and reliability" and asking himself, "Where are the contradictions? Do the conclusions make sense in the real world? What are the flaws (all research is flawed) and how could those flaws be overcome in future research?"[10]

These questions are important because academic reading inevitably leads to academic writing. Most courses in doctoral and academically oriented master's programs require students to write a final paper, as well as complete smaller writing assignments throughout the semester. Sometimes this final paper reports on research conducted during the course. Other times, the final paper is a proposal for research that a student might conduct in the future, perhaps over winter break or in the summer.[11] In either case, as English scholars Gerald Graff and Cathy Birkenstein explain in *They Say, I Say: The Moves that Matter in Academic Writing*, graduate students need to be able to articulate the point or overall findings that a work presents and conceptualize their own responses. "[T]he underlying structure of effective academic writing—and of responsible public discourse—resides not just in stating our own ideas but in listening closely to others around us, summarizing their views in a way that they will recognize, and responding with our own ideas in kind."[12]

Graduate school papers and projects are not, however, merely an exercise in creating something that can be graded. Master's student projects can serve as applications to address real-world problems. Master's theses can help master's students gain admission to PhD programs, and PhD course papers can, indirectly, help PhD students find faculty positions. PhD students typically revise course papers and turn them into submissions to local, regional or national conferences. The best of those conference presentations, in turn, are submitted to peer-reviewed journals (one journal at a time), building the publication and presentation record that PhD graduates must have to be attractive to universities or research institutes seeking tenure-track faculty or postdoctoral fellows.

Because graduate students, especially those in PhD programs, are playing a long game, organization is important. You may need to cite in your exams, thesis, project or dissertation some of the texts that you studied in the first week of the first course in your program. So finding a system for archiving what you read is important. Some students keep lists of relevant readings in a spreadsheet. Others link PDF versions of readings to entries in online citation managers such as Mendeley, Zotero, EndNote or RefWorks. Still others keep folders of related readings in the cloud, labeled by course or topic. Whatever your method, there is a tremendous value in employing it religiously.

The need to understand texts, complete courses and publish research can leave graduate students, particularly doctoral students, feeling anxious. As much as possible, says Christoph Mergerson, at this writing a fourth-year student in the PhD program in the School of Communication and Information at Rutgers University, graduate students should try to avoid putting pressure on themselves:

> Stereolab once sang, "Don't let anyone hurt your heart." Apply that advice to a doctoral program. Don't get so wrapped up in the pressures and stresses of being a doctoral student that you lose perspective of the fact that you have an opportunity to become a world-class expert about the thing that excites you

the most. Don't let the process that comes with all of that hurt your heart. Don't overly stress about grades and exams. Don't overly stress about being perfect, especially when the inevitable setbacks or bad days or weeks come (and they will). Don't compare yourself to others, whether you think they're doing well or not.

TAKING COMPREHENSIVE/QUALIFYING EXAMS

That's good advice, too, for taking the required exams that come at the end of graduate coursework. Many graduate programs of all kinds, and virtually all U.S. PhD programs in media and communication fields, require students to take exams at the end of their coursework. These exams can be divided into two broad types: comprehensive exams and qualifying exams.

Comprehensive exams, the form used by most master's programs that have exams, as well as many PhD programs, look backward, testing students, *comprehensively*, on what they learned in coursework. Sometimes all students in a program take similar comprehensive exams, covering material that faculty members believe is canonical. In other programs, each student selects (in consultation with an advisor) a specific combination of subject areas the exams will cover. My own PhD exams took this format. I took comprehensive exams in five areas—media ethics, media law, First Amendment theory, qualitative methods and quantitative methods—answering one question per area, without the use of any outside resources, over five days.

In contrast, qualifying exams, used by some PhD programs, look forward, toward the dissertation. They ask students to demonstrate that they are *qualified* to do the work of writing a dissertation proposal and a dissertation. Rather than focus on coursework, these exams home in more tightly on the theories, concepts or methods that will be foundational to a doctoral student's dissertation. The PhD program in which I teach uses this type of exam, with students tested on two areas of their choice in which they will need deep knowledge to write a dissertation, such as political economy of the media and gender, race and class and media. Each student gets ten days, with unlimited access to scholarly resources, to write two papers of about 25 pages each in answer to two questions, one from each area.

Preparation for exams can take weeks or even months. For comprehensive exams, students thoroughly review and synthesize coursework concepts and literature relevant to their tested areas. Qualifying exams often require students to delve into new literature they need to cite for their dissertations. The key in either case is to make sure your committee members have agreed on what work you should review or read for the first time. Then set out a specific amount of time for reviewing the material from each course (in the case of comprehensive exams) or reading (in the case of qualifying exams), working backward from the month or date when you expect to start writing the exam.

Because there is a lot riding on comprehensive or qualifying exams—they determine whether you advance to *candidacy* and can finish your program—you should clear your schedule as much as possible when you take them. If you're working full-time while in graduate school, it's a good idea to take a few vacation days during exams. If you're the teacher-of-record for a course, exam time is a good time to schedule a guest lecture (by a colleague from your cohort, perhaps, for whom you'll do the same favor later), show a film or present lecture material that you are very familiar with. It's very common to be anxious during this process. I slept badly and became convinced that I knew nothing about one of my areas. You *will* survive.

After you finish writing, the resulting work will be read by your committee, usually made up of four faculty members, who may become part of your thesis or dissertation committee. Then, in cooperation with your advisor, you schedule a meeting known as an oral defense. (Finding a time for five people to meet may be one of the most difficult tasks of your grad school life!) During this event, which might last an hour to two hours, members of the exam committee will ask you about the written responses, seeking to clarify assertions that were fuzzy or asking you to further explicate especially intriguing portions of the answers. If there were deficiencies in your written answer—one I see often is that students provide a thorough review of scholarly perspectives on a topic but don't themselves take a position—your committee will see if you can articulate an oral response that fills in the gaps.

Possible outcomes vary by university and program. In many programs, however, a student can:

- **Pass the exams**, becoming a master's or PhD *candidate*.
- **Be forced to rewrite all or part of the exams** and have a second oral defense of the new versions.
- **Fail the exams.** In some PhD programs, this is the last point at which students can be forced to leave the program. (A student who cannot pass comprehensive or qualifying exams cannot go on to work on a dissertation, in most cases.)

If you have passed exams, you are ready to move on to the next step in most graduate school programs: writing a master's thesis or dissertation, which you will learn more about in chapter 6.

SUMMARY

To recap, from the time you decide to go to graduate school to the time you graduate, you will be making a series of choices and fulfilling a series of requirements. The best way to start making those choices and understanding those requirements is by doing what you're doing at this very minute by reading this book: gathering relevant information. Once you have some background knowledge, you can turn to others for help. You do this when you build a relationship with a master's or PhD advisor, who can guide you in the required parts of your graduate school life: selecting courses and preparing for comprehensive or qualifying exams and completing a project, thesis or dissertation.

NOTES

[1] Niraj Chokshi, "Myspace, Once the King of Social Networks, Lost Years of Data from its Heydey," *The New York Times*, March 19, 2019. Available at https://www.nytimes.com/2019/03/19/business/myspace-user-data.html; Nicholas Jackson & Alexis C. Madigral, "The Rise and Fall of MySpace," TheAtlantic.com, January 12, 2011. Available at https://www.theatlantic.com/technology/archive/2011/01/the-rise-and-fall-of-myspace/69444/.

[2] Robert L. Peters, *Getting What You Came For: The Smart Student's Guide to Earning a Master's or Ph.D.*, rev. ed. (New York: Farrar, Straus and Giroux, 1997).

[3] Benita J. Barnes, Elizabeth A. Williams & Shuli Arieh Archer, "Characteristics That Matter Most: Doctoral Students' Perceptions of Positive and Negative Advisor Attributes," *NACADA Journal*, 30, no. 1 (spring 2010): 34–46.

[4] Michael J. Hilmer and Christiana E. Hilmer, "Is It Where You Go or Who You Know? On the Relationship Between Students, PhD Program Quality, Dissertation Advisor Prominence, and Early Career Publishing Success," *Economics of Education Review*, 30, no. 5 (October 2011): 991–996.

[5] Jonathan Grove, "PhDs: 'Toxic Supervisors' and 'Students from Hell,'" TimesHigher Education.com, April 7, 2016. Available at https://www.timeshighereducation.com/news/phds-toxic-supervisors-and-students-from-hell; Isaiah Hankel, "What to Do When Your Academic Advisor Mistreats You," CheekyScientist.com (n.d.). Available at https://cheekyscientist.com/academic-advisor/.

[6] "Bad PhD Supervisors Can Ruin Research. So Why Aren't They Accountable?," *The Guardian*, December 11, 2015. Available at https://www.theguardian.com/higher-education-network/2015/dec/11/bad-phd-supervisors-can-ruin-research-so-why-arent-they-accountable.

[7] David Demeritt, "Research Training and the End(s) of the PhD," *Geoforum* 35 (2004), 655–660; Maresi Narad & Mimi Heggelund (Eds.), *Toward a Global PhD? Forces and Forms in Doctoral Education Worldwide* (Seattle: University of Washington Press, 2008).

[8] Chrissie Boughey, "Learning to Research: A 'Social' Account," in Petro du Preez & Shan Simmonds (Eds.), *A Scholarship of Doctoral Education: On Becoming a Researcher*, 171–191 (Capetown, South Africa: African Sun Press, 2018), p. 185.

[9] Kevin P. Taylor, "How to Read Like a Doctoral Student," Founder/Scholar.com. Available at http://www.founderscholar.com/how-to-read-doctoral-student/.

[10] Ibid.
[11] Papers that are proposals for studies are especially popular in subfields or courses where research involving humans, rather than media forms, is required. Students who want to do research involving what are referred to as "human subjects," i.e., people, often cannot get university institutional review board approval for this work in time for them to conduct a study and analyze the data it produces before a traditional 15-week fall or spring semester is over.
[12] Gerald Graff & Cathy Birkenstein, *They Say; I Say: Moves That Matter in Academic Writing* (New York: W. W. Norton, 2018), 3.

4

Getting the Most Out of Your Graduate Assistantship

Amanda Sturgill, Elon University

Congratulations on receiving a graduate assistantship! It's a chance for you to pay the bills, helping you get your degree, of course. But your assistantship is much more. It's a chance for you to apprentice at tasks you may be doing for the rest of your career. Skills I acquired as a graduate assistant I am using today in my career as a professor. Being a graduate assistant can help you both to get your first job and to feel more confident as you do it. Although you can learn a great deal from the experience of an assistantship, it's up to you to make sure you seek important experiences and learn from them.

One of the trickiest parts of being a graduate student is balancing your own studies with the work that you do to pay for them. It's easy to feel overwhelmed when you are helping students review for a test while trying to prepare for your own or are stuck on campus running subjects in an experiment at inconvenient hours. But your work as a graduate assistant is more than a chance for you to support your studies. It's a chance to learn and develop as the professional you will be when you graduate with your degree. In this chapter, you will learn about strategies for not just surviving your assistantship but getting all that you can out of it so it will help you develop toward your future career.

Whether you will be grading undergraduate papers or writing research papers for publication, your work as a graduate assistant offers you some great opportunities. The first are obviously financial. The university is making a substantial investment in you by providing not only a stipend, but also usually providing the cost of tuition to make it possible to complete your graduate studies. For most graduate students, the stipend is not a tremendous sum. I remember in graduate school having to think carefully about what I could afford at the grocery store or how high I could raise the thermostat in Upstate New York winters. Although it's easy to think of an assistantship as poverty wages, being a teaching and then research assistant did allow me to finish my doctorate without student debt. Remember the value of your degree itself!

Ideally, you'll find out the parameters of your assistantship at the time that you are accepted to graduate school. In some cases, you'll find out closer to the start of the semester if the university hasn't completed its budget process at the time you are accepted. In that case, you'll know that you will have support, but you won't know exactly what you are doing. Assistantships come in different types, with different expectations. Here are some common ones:

The research assistantship: Assisting faculty members with any aspects of scholarly work including library and writing work, designing studies, running studies, working with data or doing analysis.

The teaching assistantship: Assisting instructors with their courses. You may be expected to grade student work, run recitation or other student learning sessions, keep office hours for students to get help, or do administrative work for classes such as making copies, charting attendance or taking notes during class sessions.

The instructor of record: Teaching at least one section of a class. Your students may be substantially younger than you or could be older, depending on the student mix at your university. You may be following a standard course plan with existing lessons and common tests, or as an advanced graduate student, you may be designing and running a class completely on your own.

Other types of assistantships: Some assistantships involve doing different kinds of tasks like running a resource center or lab for help for students and/or faculty and staff, managing storage and access to equipment for teaching or research, or helping with department administration. Sometimes, these assistantships are not in the same department where you are studying.

GETTING ORIENTED TO PROCEDURES

Across positions, it's important to get a handle on the scope of your job. Your graduate director or supervisor should be able to share basics like how many hours per week you are expected to work, how to track of those hours and get paid, and what period of time the assistantship covers. For example, find out if you are expected to work over university holidays and vacations. You will need to find out what your physical workspace will be like. It's common to share a department office with either other teaching or research assistants or to have a desk in your mentor's lab. Learning about the university computing systems to keep track of grades or data, and the training available, may be part of the orientation process. Additionally, you'll learn what access you need for your job, which may include printers, copy machines, databases, tutoring rooms and more. If you can, ask an experienced grad student for a tour.

For teaching assistants and instructors of record, your first order of business is finding out the tasks that you will be doing and when they will happen. Are you expected to attend class sessions? If so, all of them? If just on certain days such as to proctor exams, when are those dates? Clarify the expectations up front so both you and the instructor can be on the same page. Likewise, research assistants should meet with their faculty supervisors to sketch out the duties and hours ahead of time.

SETTING UP YOUR WORK

Communication

I found that managing my schedule was one of the trickier parts of being a graduate assistant, particularly when teaching. When I was a grader for someone else, I was subject to the class due dates. The students would turn something in, and then it was my job to have it turned around and graded by the next week. As a research assistant, I sometimes had to plan my work around grant or conference paper deadlines. Now, as a faculty member who has worked with graduate students, a lot of issues revolve around understanding expectations. Your life will be easier if you are proactive about this. You will want to establish the best way to communicate with the others involved in your assistantship. How and when is the best way to contact your supervisor? You should ask this question directly of the supervisor—not all faculty are good about using e-mail and some prefer frequent updates, whereas others will only want to know when there are problems. You should also know how the supervisor expects to communicate with you. If you are used to texting, but your supervisor prefers e-mail, or messages sent through the learning management system, make plans to check regularly. If you have others that you work with such as members of a research lab or other teaching assistants for the same course, you will want to establish ways to communicate with them as well.

It's also helpful to think about your work environment in terms of both items you need for your job and items you need for your own studies. For example, if you will be waiting long hours in a research lab to accommodate appointments to run subjects for an experiment, bring materials to work on your own courses during downtime. If you are a teaching assistant holding office hours for a copyediting class, it would be helpful to have a stylebook and dictionary at your desk to use when working with students. Talking with other assistants in your situation can help you to think through what your days will be like so you can be prepared.

Time Management

Managing your time well is necessary as a graduate assistant. Although you will probably have a job that lists a certain number of hours per week, often, the hours don't work out to be so even. You will have deadlines in both your studies and your assistantship and you will need to think ahead to be able to manage both. There are multiple calendars that you will need to reconcile. First, at some universities, the graduate program and the undergraduate program do not run on exactly the same calendar. Start and end dates may differ, as may exam schedules and things like spring break. The undergraduate calendar may interact with your assistantship whether you are teaching or using undergraduates as research participants or undergraduate lab assistants. If you are working with undergraduate classes, their schedule may affect yours on a weekly basis.

Generally, your supervisor will expect you to arrange your own schedule to accommodate the needs of the class or the lab. Consider the schedule of assignments and exams for the undergraduate courses you assist, as they can affect you in several ways. If you are expected to hold office hours, monitor online discussions or provide other support, expect your time demands to increase shortly before exams or major assignments are due. After the exam or assignment is completed, you may be expected to spend many hours grading. If your undergraduates have an exam or you have to do a lot of lab hours the same week as a major paper due for your own class, this can present a major problem. It is up to you to anticipate these issues by looking ahead in both calendars. Then work early on some of the tasks to free up time to grade student assignments (for which the timing may be out of your control). Avoid scheduling conflicts by planning ahead and addressing them early. For example, if your supervisor wants you to proctor exams at the same time as you have an exam for your own class, you can usually know this as soon as you have the syllabi for both. That time, at the start of the semester, is when you should be working with both professors to resolve the conflict by trading proctoring duties with another teaching assistant or potentially taking your graduate exam at a different time. If you are committed to go to a conference that will make grading an assignment or test rapidly difficult, address that conflict as soon as you know about it. Control what you can by working ahead and communicate early about what you can't.

Finally, it's important to consider your own energy levels. I found that some types of work like grading tests or quizzes with a key didn't require much of me. I'm most productive first thing in the morning, so I'd save that time for harder things like working on my own reading or homework and use my sluggish early afternoon for more mundane tasks like entering grades or formatting references for a grant. If there are parts of your assistantship that you really hate doing (coding data for me), see if you can schedule work time with a friend in the grad office or a nice coffee shop. I found that camaraderie helped made the drudge work pass more quickly. It can also be handy to have someone to bounce ideas off of as you are assessing a student's argument or assigning codes for a research paper.

USING YOUR TIME AS AN ASSISTANT TO DEVELOP AS A PROFESSIONAL

Many graduate degrees holders will end up teaching during their careers. Teaching assistantships offer the chance to learn and practice skills and to consider a philosophy of teaching that you'll need later for faculty job applications. If at all possible, it's useful to attend class sessions and examine the reading or other materials students use for the class. You can then get insights about how what happens in the class affects student learning. A teaching assistant will commonly help with assessing student work and with helping address student questions. It's worth it for you to take time when grading to note the types of errors that are made most frequently—what exam questions students were most likely to get wrong, or what writing errors are common. Use that information to see if the weak performance is the result of the structure of the assignment itself, for example an ambiguous exam question or a poorly worded assignment. If it is not, you can see what happened in the class or the readings that might cause the students to have had difficulty learning those concepts.

When it comes to handling student concerns or answering questions, whether you are a teaching assistant or an instructor of record, it can be useful to note the types of concerns students have and when you hear about them. For example, if several students ask for extensions on a particular assignment, consider if they have the knowledge to complete the assignment or how the assignment falls in the rhythms of the academic term. If students complain about team members in group projects, you might think about how to provide support in group process that will allow groups to work together more harmoniously and effectively. If you get many requests for help by e-mail late at night, you might consider if instructors need to educate students about boundaries and reasonable expectations. In all of these cases, deliberately reflecting on the ways students react and perform in the context of what happens in the class can help you see big-picture strategies that will work when you are in charge of planning courses by yourself.

Research assistants can also benefit from incorporating reflection in action as they complete their duties for their jobs. For example, one task research assistants sometimes have is finding supporting literature for work the lab is doing. You'll do this in a targeted way in your classes as well. The assistantship can be a good chance to learn a citation management tool like EndNote, RefWorks or Zotero to help you keep up with the major ideas in fields you might research. Research assistants also commonly work with participants to collect data, by administering surveys, running experiments, etc. If you are part of a larger lab with many types of studies, see if you can help with or observe data collection in multiple modalities so you can get firsthand exposure to the benefits and limitations of various methods. You can also learn about supervising others if you are managing the work of undergraduate assistants who are directly collecting the data. Sometimes assistants will code for content or thematic analysis. This can be a chance to note and reflect on the types of coder training that make a difference in accuracy of coding across coders.

At research-focused universities, two metrics will matter a great deal for tenure: citation of your work and ability to win external research grants. Take the opportunity of your assistantship to thoroughly understand the research process. Even if you are not the first author of a publication, still see if you are able to see letters of transmittal, what external reviewer reports look like, the process of approving proofs and so on. If your lab is funded by grants, this can be a great opportunity to see how grants are found and the application process. Even if you are not submitting your own large grant applications, you can still be involved in preparing them through finding literature or other information, proofreading and other steps. Direct involvement in grant applications will be an asset in job interviews. With all of these research experiences, don't be afraid to ask questions about what is going on.

Sometimes assistants are doing other jobs in the university or even off campus, like working as office support staff. Even there, there are some valuable lessons you can learn. The primary one is about the structure of the university itself. You can observe how support staff work together to enable the teaching, scholarship and public service that may be at the heart of the university's mission. This type of understanding can be valuable for future university service obligations during your career.

SPECIAL CONCERNS FOR TEACHING ASSISTANTS

When you are preparing to be a teaching assistant, it's important that you fully understand the course you are supporting. That means being familiar with the topics and tasks of the course for students (What will they learn about? How will this learning be measured? What will they do in class and out?). Courses will have learning goals for the students, and you should know what those are so you can plan your work to ensure those goals are met. For example, if you are supporting a screenwriting class, you'll need to understand formatting guidelines for screenplays. You should be very familiar with the syllabus as well as the material being taught in class sessions. If you are not already well versed in the topic, this may mean doing readings or practicing with technology or techniques before the students are expected to. One good idea is to offer to review assignment descriptions before they are given to the students. Sometimes the faculty member benefits from having a student's view of the task as described, and it ensures that you, as the assistant, have a good understanding so you can help students if they have issues.

Be prepared on logistics as well. Any time you are meeting a group of students on your own, whether that's a review session in a classroom, tutoring in the library or staffing a software lab, newsroom or studio, check the room out thoroughly before the first time you meet the students. Figure out how to gain access to the room, how the projection technology works, what kind of boards there are, how to darken the room if needed, and if the furniture can be configured to support different kinds of discussions (moving into a circle or U to encourage face-to-face discussion, for example). You don't want to discover that your ID does not open the electronic lock while standing out in the cold surrounded by students at the first recitation session. You should also know how to exit the building in case of emergency and have an emergency plan in place for fire alarms. Find out if you should call 911 or campus police. An administrative assistant who works in the building can probably help you get this information.

Tips for Teaching Assistants

- Have a "teaching" tote. As you realize what you need to bring to class (whiteboard markers, extra printer paper, a stapler, a jacket because it is always cold or whatever), designate a bag or backpack for just that class. Put a folder with the attendance list, syllabus and class handouts in it. Bring the bag with you to every section, and you will always have what you need.

- Take attendance. You might be required to do so by the university. Either way, it lets students know you care that they are there and, in case of an emergency, confirm that everyone is out of the building.
- Check out other textbooks. If you are looking for examples to use when reviewing things for students, other textbooks on the same content area can be a good source.
- Create notes for yourself. If you come across examples you know will be good later in the semester, throw a link in the learning management system (Blackboard, Moodle, Canvas, etc.) and make it hidden from students. That way you can find it later.
- Take advantage of any teaching training the university offers to grad students. If your department doesn't offer training, ask your graduate director is there is a university-wide program or if they can arrange for you to attend the training that is offered by another department. Sometimes great ideas come from training for TAs for science, business or liberal arts.
- Grade wisely. When assessing work, remember that sometimes less is more. A smaller number of big-picture comments is easier to digest than a hemorrhage of red ink correcting every little thing in the paper. Students can always meet with you about their papers if they have questions.
- Learn more about teaching. If you are the professor of record for a class, the book *Master Class: Teaching Advice for Journalism and Mass Communication Instructors* is a complete guide to the teaching process written by members of AEJMC's Standing Committee on Teaching.[1]

SPECIAL CONCERNS FOR RESEARCH ASSISTANTS

Research assistantships also have their own set of expectations and duties. When you start a research assistantship, it's important to get up to speed on the parameters of the research. This includes two major aspects: the theoretical basis for the studies and the methods that are used. Methods generally includes how data is collected, how it is analyzed and how it is presented to the public. Your own graduate classes will cover the basics of how to do research of various types, but you should expect to need to read on your own for the particulars of the scholarship for your job. The types of scholarship vary quite a bit in communication. Assistants could be doing anything from production assisting on a documentary to attaching leads to measure research participants' heart rates. Where possible, your assistantship will match with your previous experiences. In this case, you mostly need to learn how to adapt those experiences to an academic setting. For example, if you created videos for an ad agency after college, you may find that some of your job will be doing background research to plan interviews or B-roll shoots for a faculty documentary. You may be figuring out solutions to making films on a tiny budget. In the same way, if you were a journalist prior to graduate school, you may still be doing interviews for a research assistantship that includes oral histories, but the types of interviews you do and the write-ups will be quite different.

One big difference between graduate school and undergraduate is that you are often expected to be substantially more independent as a graduate student. This means that if you don't know how to do something, you will be expected to make substantial progress toward figuring it out on your own. The faculty that you work with can give you some direction, but you should be prepared to ask other graduate students, look up articles and videos and so on to find out what you need to know to do your job. Sometimes the techniques will be covered in your graduate classes. In any case, in order to be effective at research, you need to be fully confident you understand the technique before you do any data collection, whether you are interviewing humans or coding articles. The same is true if you are expected to do analysis of collected data. Many colleges and universities have on-campus statistical consulting that may be useful when planning for how to tackle data analysis.

Tips for Research Assistants

- Get to know the librarian who supports your area. They can be a valuable resource.
- Keep good notes about your research process. They are useful for methods sections later and for preparing for job talks.
- If your job involves running experiments, confirm with your participants the day of.
- Do invest the time in learning a citation management program and putting everything you cite into it. What is time consuming at first will save you a lot of time later.
- If you can, synergize by choosing class project work that is related to your assistantship.

DEALING WITH ANXIETY

Imposter syndrome is when you fear that you are not capable of doing what is asked of you and terrified that others will find out. It is pernicious in academia and particularly relevant to graduate students.

Your assistantship is a prime vector for imposter syndrome as you are being asked to teach students occupying desks you were very recently in yourself or helping to create publishable research with techniques you are only just learning. It can also be frustrating because while the undergraduate experience is usually full of frequent assessment and feedback, the assistantship portion of your graduate experience likely will not be. You may only hear feedback from your supervisor when things go wrong, and this can feel demoralizing.

One issue that graduate assistants may struggle with is power and authority when they work with others. You may feel awkward acting like you are able to manage, advise or even help them, particularly when the things you are working with are relatively new to you as well. Remember that even if the difference between what you know and what they know is not great, it is still a difference and a difference that matters. Graduate assistants are often great at helping undergraduates to master material because they have learned it recently themselves and know the strategies that worked for them. When it comes to work in a research program, just having a handle on the big picture of the research allows you to provide guidance and a framework for the work others are doing.

THE DANGER ZONE

There are a few areas that can be real pitfalls for graduate assistants. These fall into categories including work with faculty supervisors, relationships with students and keeping records. In all of these cases, your actions and the interactions that you have with others can have a lasting impact on both your time in graduate school and your long-term career.

When it comes to work with faculty supervisors, you can have issues with assignments, relationships, research project credit and other issues. Inappropriate assignments refer to tasks outside of the scope of university work. For example, some professors have gotten in trouble for asking graduate assistants to provide childcare or to do yard work at a faculty member's home. These kinds of personal favors clearly violate one of the goals of your assistantship: to give you the chance to develop professional skills that you will use in your career. Because your stipend, tuition and in some cases immigration status depend on you keeping your supervisor happy, you may be tempted to accede to these requests. It is a bad idea to do this, if for no other reason because the time spent is time you have already stretched thin meeting your own academic and your assistantship obligations. It is also a bad idea because it could be a liability problem if you were to become injured or even inadvertently cause injury in the course of doing tasks like these. As a director of graduate studies, it was my job to keep up with situations like this and to address them with the relevant faculty member. You, too, should consult with the director of your graduate program if something like that happens to you. If the person making the inappropriate request IS the director of the graduate program, the department chair would be the appropriate person. If your university has an ombudsman for students (search on the university website), they could also provide advice on how to handle situations like this.

There have also been cases of faculty seeking inappropriate romantic relationships with graduate students. Most universities have policies against faculty–student relationships, but in some cases, issues with graduate students are not taken as seriously. They should be, because the issues are the same. Even if you are interested in this kind of relationship, it's a bad idea while you are in school because it is influenced by the teacher-student power dynamic that allows for free and fair assessment of the student's work. If you are not interested, it is even worse, as you may feel pressured to cooperate because the faculty member holds sway over your continuation in the program. Both of these kinds of issues need you as the student to get help in dealing with them. If a polite "no" does not work, you should consult with your graduate program director for support. If this does not provide help or if the problem is the graduate program director, the staff of the university's graduate school or the department chair of your unit would be the next option. Universities face substantial liability, particularly for inappropriate relationships, and university staff should want to hear your story and help you.

Be mindful of boundaries in relationships with students as well. Often, students you work with are close to your age. This can cause problems, as students feel like their familiarity to you entitles them to special relationships or privileges like assuming you'll be understanding of their challenging schedules when they turn work in late. The best solution for this is clear policies. If you don't take late work, be consistent on this with every student, every time. You can blame the policy (even though you made it) for what feels to the student like an unkind decision. Sometimes students think they can have a social relationship with grad assistants because the age difference is minimal. This is not a good idea, as it can cause problems when you have to issue grades or make decisions that affect them. It can lead to charges of favoritism, or even inadvertently, to favoritism itself. It is never appropriate for a graduate student to date or have a romantic relationship with an undergraduate student in the same academic area. This is especially important if the graduate student has now or may ever have any kind of academic relationship with the student. Your department likely has policies about such relationships, and you can ask your graduate director about this. Graduate students should also be careful about other social situations with undergraduates. For example, it could be problematic for grad students to end up at events with underage drinking or any kind of substance use. Be especially careful if your situation requires you to travel away from the campus with students. Just because the venue changes doesn't mean your relationships do.

When it comes to credit for authorship on manuscripts written as part of your assistantship, there are standards of the field. Basically, only people who do work on a project should be listed and, in communication fields, authorship is in order based on the contributions each person makes to the project. This contribution refers to the contribution to the substance, not just the time spent. For example, if a student spends hours supervising participants in an experiment but does nothing toward designing the experiment or writing the paper, they would likely not be an author. They contributed time, but not substance to the manuscript. Good practice is to have explicit conversations about authorship at the time that a study is designed. Not all supervisors take the initiative, though. It is in your best interest to broach the subject if the supervisor does not. A conversation at the beginning can alleviate concern and unhappiness later. Also, just because an advisor is more prominent in the field does not mean that they should necessarily be the first author, if they do not make the major contribution.

It's important that as a part of your duties, you are careful to make and keep records in legally correct and helpful ways. If you are a research assistant, information about study participants is governed by laws relating to the conduct of research. If you deal with human participants at all, you'll probably be asked to undergo training for the protection of their rights in research. If you are not asked to complete a training course, ask about it. There are online courses that offer certifications and are not arduous. They serve as a good background for decision-making today and for your future. In particular, be careful about storing data in a way that keeps it confidential—for example, leaving it on your password-free laptop in your shared office could allow other people to access it. Also, you can't discuss who participates in studies with others.

When it comes to student data like grades, there are also applicable laws. You may be assigning grades and entering them, or you may be responsible for all the grading in a class. In either case, all the information about student performance is confidential and should only be shared with those in the university who need to know. One particular area of concern is parents, who sometimes try to contact academic staff with questions about how their son or daughter is doing in courses. You are not legally able to answer these questions unless the student has signed paperwork waiving their right to privacy for these records. You need confirmation of that from the university registrar—the word of the student or the parent is not sufficient as they don't always remember.

THE FRUITFUL ASSISTANTSHIP

Regardless of the type of assistantship, I'd encourage you to use this experience as a chance to become a reflective practitioner. Take the time to regularly take some notes about the experience. What did you do? How well did it work? What did you learn that might help you do better next time? If possible, take advantage of chances to share with others who do things differently. Can you observe in the classes of a variety of professors at your school? Would some of the researchers let you sit in on a lab meeting? Academia is known for its intense time commitments during the term, but there are also the times in between the terms where you can take a few hours to think about the bigger picture of your assistantship and what you are learning that you will use in your career. This will pay large benefits as you are preparing to go on the job market, as you will have ready answers for what you do well and how you address areas where you still need to grow. This will truly let you get the maximum out of being a graduate assistant.

NOTE

[1] Standing Committee on Teaching, *Master Class: Teaching Advice for Journalism and Mass Communication Instructors*, edited by Chris Roush (Lanham, MD: Rowman & Littlefield, 2018).

5

The Mindful Thesis or Dissertation

Finding the Focus to Write

Jan Lauren Boyles, Iowa State University

You will never forget your thesis or dissertation defense date. Trust me.

For me, it started with a service delay on Washington, D.C.'s Red Line Metro system, which I used for the 45-minute commute back-and-forth to American University's campus. Running late, I began the day by staining my fancy new suit with my morning coffee. I subsequently spilled a box of pastries (purchased for my dissertation co-chairs and committee members) on the campus shuttle. (Yes, some of the undergrads aboard the shuttle didn't care and ate them anyway. I thought my professors, on the other hand, probably wouldn't want bus floor donuts). Surely, these events were signs—collective omens—that my dissertation defense was simply doomed and destined for failure.

But that's the moment it all changed.

I had invited friends and colleagues to attend my defense. One by one, they arrived in the conference room. Spectators flowed into the hallway, leaving little space for my committee members. Instead of stage fright, I felt the camaraderie and support emanating from everyone in that room. The dissertation journey would not have been possible without those cheerleaders.

While writing a thesis or dissertation requires months (and yes, perhaps years) of solitude, nobody writes one alone. Chairs supervise. Committee members counsel. Classmates support. Loved ones listen. And none of these people want to see you fail. Navigating the writing process to completion requires careful and methodical planning, however. The initial steps may seem overwhelming. Where, on earth, do you begin? The defense date may loom so far into the distance that it seems unattainable. Do not let this endless jumble of to-do lists cloud your vision. Simply stated, scholarly writing mandates mindfulness. It requires being fully aware and present in the moment—whether that's listening to an interviewee, carefully coding content or gathering feedback from your chair. Progressing through each stage of the writing process necessitates dedicated focus. In this chapter, I highlight strategies to achieve and maintain the level of strategic concentration needed to write your thesis or dissertation.

NARROWING THE SCOPE

One of the initial challenges in crafting a thesis or dissertation rests in defining the study's central research vision. Honestly speaking, blazing a new trail for your research idea often starts with a period of wandering through the academic wilderness. This process generally begins by meandering through endless sets of academic database queries to fully understand the scholarly work that has been previously published on your thesis or dissertation subject. Registering for e-mail alerts from academic journals can help with tracking the latest advances in your subfield. As you progress through your graduate degree program, class papers may serve as jumping off points to explore the literature, serving to ultimately narrow the focus of your own research project. (For doctoral students eyeing tenure-track employment, revising these papers can also be valuable toward establishing a publication track record in peer-reviewed journals.) At this stage, accessing prior theses or dissertations from your institution may also assist in defining how much ground your study should cover.

This "wilderness walk" through the literature doesn't have to occur in isolation, however. When I was first starting to write my dissertation, my doctoral co-chair recommended that I reach out to three aspirational scholars for ten-minute conversations on the state of my subfield. The intention of these exchanges was not to talk specifically about my dissertation topic but rather to learn from the best and the brightest about the current landscape of the discipline itself. I sent e-mails to arrange those conversations. I can't begin to tell you how nervous I felt in placing those calls. But I was pleasantly overwhelmed by the kindness of senior scholars in journalism studies, who were delighted to talk about their research. These exchanges helped me refine my ideas on how my research could address blind spots within the scholarly canon.

Once a solid command of the current state of scholarship has been grasped, you will begin to see how your research can best fit into the discipline. Constructing the design of your thesis or dissertation will require trade-offs. Selecting ethnography as a method, for instance, may be time consuming to secure access to the field site, but ultimately yield valuable data. Expanding your study's sample size may require financial support to incentivize participants. In designing your thesis or dissertation, it is important to fully weigh such methodological alternatives. At this point, you and your advisor should also develop strong parameters on what your study will—and more importantly, will not—encompass. But what is the ideal balance between an academically rigorous and a reasonably manageable thesis or dissertation? For most graduate students, this is a very tough call. Hopefully, your chair and your committee will help collaboratively shape these contours with you, keeping in mind the ever-important timeline toward graduation. In writing a thesis or dissertation, time is often your most precious commodity. In my case, I initially proposed conducting ethnographic fieldwork in three separate cities. Looking back, this idea would have been disastrous. I probably would have graduated in 2052. After considering my abbreviated timeline and limited funding, I quickly realized that delving deeper into a single case study location would provide sufficient (and rich) data for the dissertation write-up and analysis. Mindfully contemplating these trade-offs can keep the end product manageable.

Wise graduate students also consider how their thesis or dissertation can act as a launching pad for postgraduate careers. External mentors in academia or industry can provide perspective about how your thesis or dissertation topic might "play" on the future job market. For doctoral students, the dissertation is most often viewed by employers as the preeminent showcase of your talents and abilities. For those seeking tenure-track careers, the research stream established in the dissertation typically generates the first publication (or more) during your assistant professor years. As a result, external feedback can further refine the dissertation's scope so that it can be leveraged as a marketable springboard for your future professional success.

DEVELOPING THE PROPOSAL

After you have identified a research topic to pursue, you will begin working more closely with your advisor and committee to refine these ideas. In addition to your thesis or dissertation chair (who will serve as the primary point person for your questions on the project), you will generally have two or more faculty members from your department who will also provide feedback as your committee members. At most institutions, you will also be asked to select an "external" member—a faculty member who is outside of your department. Their role is to provide an independent lens on the research. Ideally, this individual should contribute complementary skills in either theory or methods that can strengthen your work from another disciplinary angle. But a word to the wise: Before extending any invites to any prospective committee members, share a proposed list with your thesis or dissertation chair. He/she/they can provide feedback not only on each member's scholarly expertise, but also on how the temperaments of your committee members might interplay with one another. The thesis or dissertation path has enough built-in stress without worrying about how committee member egos might collectively wrangle in intellectual fistfights. To this end, I also recommend that students meet one-on-one with prospective committee members. In most cases, these meetings will give you an immediate sense if your personalities mesh or if the faculty member has excellent insights to add to your work. You have veto power here. If you don't feel like a committee member is a good fit, it's perfectly acceptable to decline their participation. Remember, at the end of the day, this is *your* thesis or dissertation—so draft faculty members who you believe will best inform and promote your research.

After the committee roster has been solidified, the next step is drafting a proposal for your thesis or dissertation. Generally, this document contains: (1) a modest literature review that demonstrates your working knowledge of prior studies in the field, (2) an overview of the theoretical framework that you would like to use, (3) a preliminary write-up of the methods that you would integrate into the project and (4) an overall timeline of how you will accomplish these tasks. Here's a secret: Dedicating more work to the proposal will ease the ultimate burden of writing your thesis or dissertation. Why? In most cases, you will repurpose this document into the thesis or dissertation itself. Be forewarned, though: It is expected that your chair will likely have several rounds of revision to the proposal. While it's always difficult to receive critical feedback, these changes are only designed to make your project stronger.

At most institutions, the next step is a proposal meeting, where your committee members gather to give feedback on your work-in-progress research. (It should be noted that some schools make this an optional step. Nevertheless, obtaining buy-in from your committee members is key to ensure your research project is on the proper course.) Perhaps the most difficult task of the entire thesis or dissertation process is finding a mutual time when your committee can assemble. Check with your committee as early as possible to block off this time in their calendars. Try to have a back-up date as well, in case any last-minute emergencies arise for your committee members.

At the proposal meeting, you will generally present a top-level overview of the project. One piece of wisdom: Students often dedicate a significant chunk of the meeting to talking about existing literature. Rather than focus on what has already been studied (research with which your committee members are already well knowledgeable), spend this time discussing how your research builds upon these studies, how your methods appropriately pair with this project and—most importantly—how your proposed project contributes to the field. After your presentation, your committee members will ask plenty of questions about your project. Again, these inquiries are just designed to spot potential problems or to extend your project's scope. Make sure that notes are recorded (either by you or your chair) to capture these points of feedback.

While it may seem stressful, everyone survives this meeting. Afterward, your heart will feel relieved because you typically now have the green light (pending IRB or other institutional approvals) to begin your thesis or dissertation work. It's now time to execute your research design. At this stage, keeping the focus on the ultimate goal of your degree is paramount. Moving from your proposal meeting to your thesis or dissertation defense just takes mindful planning.

ADHERING TO YOUR TIMELINE

Once the boundaries of the work have been mutually established with your committee, strategically setting personal "deadlines" can prove valuable. Notice that the word "deadlines" is in quotes. Academia stands apart from other industries because the work is so often self-motivated and self-driven, without clear due dates or tasks directly assigned by supervisors. Institutional graduation dates should be the starting point for crafting a writing timetable. From here, add specific "internal" (Institutional Review Board approval, for instance) and "external" (grant application due dates, for example) deadlines to the calendar. Each chair has a slightly different style in mentoring students through the writing process. Some chairs will set these target deadlines—coaching step-by-step when and how the work should progress. But in many (if not, most) cases, thesis and dissertation chairs will trust the student to submit writings without specific prompting or without reminders. Many professors consider dissertation writing, in particular, as a crucible toward future independent work in the academy. For writing productivity to thrive, freedom must be balanced with discipline. In this case, setting "artificial" due dates can keep your project on track.

A universal truth of academic writing, however, is that each and every stage of the process will take longer than expected. Delays *will* happen. This is perfectly normal and should be programmed into the writing timetable. Time should be allocated, for instance, for committee members to read drafts and provide feedback—anticipating that there may be snags in faculty availability (especially during summer terms). In this planning process, considering "Plan B" options upfront may also save precious time down the road. Proactively planning for possible problems that might crop up—such as if the survey sample size is too small, key interviewees decline participation or fieldwork sites prohibit access—can preserve the writing timeline if and when these issues occur.

Prewriting and "pre-thinking" before formally launching the thesis or dissertation will also prove beneficial. Starting too early without a clear plan for data collection and analysis can lead to duplicated and wasted effort, in some cases. Beyond the standard pretesting of interview questions or survey protocols, revisiting the literature around your thesis or dissertation topic may be a useful exercise to see how the proposed work now fits within the larger body of scholarship in your subfield. Since finishing the proposal, new studies may have been published that complement your work. Remaining in touch with recent scholarship can also help demonstrate how your thesis or dissertation builds upon and extends current research.

At this stage, I received another bit of great advice: Identify one or two writing heroes/heroines. Find academics in your subfield whose overall writing style is accessible, yet scholarly in tone. In reviewing their work, think about how they convey specialized content for broader comprehension. In my first few years on the tenure track, I struggled with finding my academic writing voice. Looking back, my early pieces feature elevated language that could have been dialed back for clearer comprehension. Simply stated, nobody wants to read a thesis or dissertation (or a journal article, monograph or book, for that matter) that needs a secret decoder ring to decipher the author's key takeaways. Constructing a thesis or dissertation using language that is smart yet grounded encourages the academic community to share your work beyond its place on a dusty library bookshelf or in a digital library repository with zero views. For doctoral students seeking an academic career, prioritizing the impact of your scholarship will become a central consideration of the progression toward tenure. For now, reading more widely across the field will help as you begin to articulate your voice as an academic writer.

SLAYING WRITING MONSTERS

After launching the project and amassing the first round of data, few things are more daunting than the computer cursor blinking on a blank page of text. But instead of directly facing the "cursor monster" lurking in the word processor, once odious tasks like cleaning out closets or mowing the lawn suddenly seem more appealing. Writing those first few words takes courage. But it also takes planning. Just like delays, writer's block is a part of the process, and should be built into the overall timeline. To combat this "monster," consider the optimal time of day when your writing brain catches fire. For me, it's early morning. To this day, I still reserve time (and a lot of coffee) between 5 and 7 a.m. for scholarly writing projects. With many competing duties in graduate student life—like serving as a teaching assistant or contributing to faculty-led scholarly projects, for example—reserving daily "do not disturb" writing time in the calendar stands essential to progress. Again, if you are seeking tenure-track life postgraduation, learning how to balance writing time now will serve as excellent practice for an academic career. The best breakthroughs on how to resolve trouble spots in academic writing, however, typically occur away from designated screen time. Taking time away from the "cursor monster" will ultimately help defeat the writing block beast.

Not every day will be a good writing day. Sometimes the words will effortlessly flow onto the screen as your fingers dance across the keys. The rush feels like boarding a rocket ship to Mars—a solitary and bold flight into the clouds that you never thought possible. And then the next day, you will reread that "genius" material. Plummeting back to earth, the text will now seem quite ordinary, dull and useless. This is normal. Resist the urge to delete this draft. Instead, save it. For every project that I write, I have dozens of files with cutting room floor remains. Several of these files have served as the catalyst for future studies. So until the degree is conferred (and even beyond), keep all these disjointed, electronic thoughts on your computer. Writing the thesis or dissertation is rarely a linear process; instead, it moves back and forth between interdisciplinary insights that you slowly learn are connected to one another. In most cases, content that seems initially irrelevant will resurface later in a new light. So don't become discouraged on days when all that emerges from your writing time is a single paragraph or sentence. It's probably a very good paragraph or a very good sentence. Cognitively, progress is still happening. With a dedicated writing regime, the good writing days and the not-so-good writing days will ultimately balance out. To this end, some scholars find setting daily or weekly writing targets (often measured by word count) beneficial. Others join writing "accountability" groups that meet face-to-face weekly. I found best success in placing deadlines on my calendar for each section of the dissertation. University writing center staff can be especially helpful in identifying the strategies that can best motivate your progress.

One of the most unexpected challenges of thesis or dissertation writing often revolves around how to process the sheer volume of data that has been generated. The raw data that serves as the basis for your final thesis or dissertation write-up may stretch across millions of tweets, thousands of news articles, hundreds of survey participants or dozens of interviews. It may even involve weaving together data obtained from multiple methods. Combing through the data output will, at first, seem like a maze. Academic writing bears even more complexity, as these findings must ultimately tie back to prior literature, theoretical constructs and research questions. One strategy: Move forward by taking a step back. Write a one-page summary of what's been learned during the thesis or dissertation work using non-specialist terms. At the end of every writing session, go back to this document. See what remains true. Add new insights. Slowly, this one-pager can become the blueprint for the primary themes in the findings sections. During this stage, developing and following a systematic approach for reviewing the data is also key. Documenting specifics on the data analysis process as it occurs is much easier than retroactively building this content from memory. For quantitative researchers, immediately memorialize in writing how the statistical tests were conducted. For qualitative researchers, constructing daily fieldnotes can order thoughts by identifying key findings and questions that arise during interviews or fieldwork. Again, these insights will ultimately form the core of your unique contribution to the literature.

Losing these ideas can be tragic. In the process of writing the thesis or dissertation, insights will happen at the strangest times and in the strangest places. Brilliance will strike in the superstore check-out queue or in the veterinarian's waiting room. With all the conceptual juggling in your mind, failing to capture these ideas as they strike often means they will be forgotten later. Whether it's sending an e-mail to yourself or adding the idea to a productivity app on your phone, establishing a routine for recording these fleeting, a-ha moments can make an incredible difference. Be wary of electronic modes of capture, though. Even more frightening than the "cursor monster," we've all heard academic horror stories about cruel "delete demons"—like corrupted digital files, computer crashes or the catastrophic disappearance of electronic work. Cloud services have made file backups more seamless than ever. Searching and retrieving this electronic data can be made even easier by using version controls when naming files, including relevant keywords and dates. The good news is that both the "cursor monster" and the "delete demon" can be defeated with cautious and mindful planning.

COMMUNICATING YOUR PROGRESS

When problems do happen, establishing and maintaining open lines of communication with your thesis or dissertation chair during the writing process is essential. Again, delays and glitches during the process will occur. While it may be stressful to share these setbacks, chairs generally have seen similar problems with prior students. If the situation is novel, the chair can tap into the wealth of campus resources for support. As a faculty member, I have yet to see a trouble- or error-free thesis or dissertation. On the other hand, the ramifications of withholding information from your chair about a potential problem could be magnified with time. Early and honest intervention is key.

Just like every chair manages student completion-to-degree differently, faculty members also diverge in how they wish to meet with graduate students during the writing and editing process. (If you have yet to select a doctoral advisor for your dissertation, this is an especially significant issue to ponder before choosing your chair. Early in the process, have a conversation with your thesis or dissertation advisor about their preferences in handling drafts of your work.) If you are conducting your research on campus, scheduling a weekly face-to-face meeting may be effective. If you are conducting fieldwork remotely, video conferencing may be useful for these weekly check-ins. During these sessions, advisors may offer only verbal feedback on your drafts. In these cases, it may be valuable to send a follow-up e-mail, chronicling highlights discussed together. In this sense, you are both on the same page with expectations moving forward. Other chairs prefer to send detailed, written feedback using track changes. In other cases, dissertation chairs may grant even more independence for your work. My advisors favored this approach. During my PhD program, I sent my co-chairs a weekly e-mail, recapping my progress. I also placed all my dissertation content on a password protected, cloud-based service that my co-chairs and committee members could access at any time. No matter the communication strategy, do not wait until the thesis or dissertation is fully formed and complete to seek comments from your chair. Rather, ask for your chair's thoughts along the way, so there are no eleventh-hour surprises for either of you.

In addition to direct assistance from your chair, many others can grant indirect support during the writing journey. Within your department, school or college, fellow cohort members can provide counsel on the process—particularly other students who have advanced to candidacy status. In addition, immediate graduates of your program (within the last five years) are uniquely positioned to help. Having just earned degrees from your institution, they can provide insights that take the department/

school/college's culture into account. Internally, many institutions also offer thesis or dissertation writing groups, which meet weekly or biweekly. These gatherings not only solidify bonds across the graduate student campus community; they also serve to provide accountability to make progress on writing goals. Externally, a wide array of mentorship opportunities is offered through AEJMC. In short, an entire network exists that can guide your success.

SAVORING THE MOMENT

While the writing process itself can be arduous, small wins do accrue along the way. Each survey fielded, each interview completed, each story analyzed—and yes, each word written—is one step closer to receiving that coveted degree. It is possible. So celebrate these accomplishments along the way. Simple and inexpensive reward systems can sustain the momentum needed to finish. Every time my dissertation co-chairs accepted one of my dissertation chapters, I celebrated by purchasing carbonated soft drinks (some call it pop or soda—take your pick) in glass bottles. For more significant landmarks, such as submitting the entire dissertation for review, dinner out with my classmates was a terrific motivator. In writing a thesis or dissertation, incremental progress matters.

The ultimate thesis or dissertation defense represents a pivotal transition point, in which you are moving beyond your position as a graduate student toward embracing your new role as a scholar. It is a time to be proud of what you have produced. It is a time to realize you likely have spent more time engaged with this research topic than anyone else in the room. Or as my dad told me, "It is a time to be confident in your abilities." This doesn't mean that you should transform into a show-off, know-it-all. But it does mean that you can talk about your thesis or dissertation with assured conviction, knowing that you have completed the absolute best work of which you are capable. Don't be nervous; this is your well-deserved moment in the spotlight to showcase what you have learned and why it matters. Savor it.

Successfully defending the thesis or dissertation merits a larger celebration. After hours of questioning at my own defense, my dissertation committee asked me to leave the room—a customary gesture for private deliberation on whether the degree should be granted or not. My friends and colleagues stayed to hear the verdict. I think the committee sequestered themselves in the conference room for two minutes or so. It felt like an eternity, though. When the door reopened, one of my dissertation chairs extended his hand to me. He then uttered perhaps three of the greatest words in the English language I've ever heard spoken.

"Congratulations, Dr. Boyles," he said.

I nearly fainted.

The hallway erupted in cheers, tears (mine) and high fives. The celebrations continued later that afternoon with more glass-bottled soft drinks. As mementos, I saved all the bottle caps acquired throughout my dissertation journey. They are now in my desk at Iowa State University, where I'm currently an assistant professor in our journalism school. I look at them from time to time when I need a little lift. And it's come full circle: When my own graduate advisees are facing tough times, I often bring out the bottle caps again for symbolic display and a heart-to-heart conversation. Years later, they still remind me that big dreams are attainable—even writing a thesis or dissertation. It just takes mindful concentration.

You will never forget your thesis or dissertation defense date. Trust me.

ACKNOWLEDGMENTS

Thanks to Drs. Michael Bugeja, Jay Newell and Laura Witzling for their insightful thoughts (and PhD memories!) related to this chapter. And thanks to my dissertation co-chairs, Drs. Declan Fahy and Matthew C. Nisbet, for their steadfast support during my PhD program.

6

Making Sense of (and Making the Most of) Academic Conferences

Jennifer Greer, University of Kentucky

My first academic conference (AEJMC, Kansas City, 1993) involved a seventeen-hour road trip driving a manual transmission, crashing at my parents' house with fellow doc students, and cramming four people into a hotel room. None of us had submitted papers (meaning no funding), so we found the cheapest way to attend, including nabbing free food at all the exhibit room breaks and socials. My most vivid memory, however, is a classmate whispering that the great media effects scholar Steve Chaffee was standing behind us in the corridor, engaged in conversation. Of course, I whipped my head around and gawked at him, clearly failing at the whole "act like you've been here before" thing. He smiled and gave a quick wave, never missing a beat. A few years later, I found myself on a phone interview with Chaffee when I was a semifinalist for a job at Stanford, where he worked at the time. I recounted that memory, and he laughed and said he'd done the same thing as a young scholar. I didn't get the job, but every time I saw Chaffee at conferences after that, he always greeted me warmly, as if we were part of the same club.

That anecdote is emblematic of the power of academic conferences to help scholars build connections and shape careers. The networks I've built attending conferences have resulted in coauthored publications, jobs, promotions, mentoring relationships (both as a mentor and a mentee), leadership opportunities, trips across the globe and lifelong friendships. I know I'm not alone in the impact conferences have had on my life, of course, as many scholars across all disciplines have shared stories of pivotal career and personal breakthroughs that germinated at academic gatherings.

To the uninitiated, it may seem that we stumbled into these situations—a tale of being in the right place at the right time. Networking at academic conferences and beyond, however, is just like any other part of an academic career. To be successful at it means setting goals, systematically planning your strategy, keeping track of what's working and what's not, and following up. I've talked with scholars who attended solely to present a paper or go to the job hub and then lamented that they found the conference to be of little value. Worse, I've seen scholars behaving in memorable ways that actually hurt their career prospects down the road.

This chapter is designed to help graduate students get the most out of their time at academic meetings, with practical tips on choosing the right conferences, prepping for your presentation, taking advantage of all the gathering has to offer, and presenting yourself in the best light. Fully investing in the academic conference experience and doing a little preparation can have long-term payoff in an academic career.

WHAT IS AN ACADEMIC CONFERENCE?

Amy M. Buddie, in an American Psychological Association article written for undergraduate students, defines an academic conference as "a one-day or multiday event during which researchers present their work to each other."[1] In an academic setting, these researchers likely are faculty members and their graduate or, increasingly, undergraduate students. At communication conferences, it is not uncommon for faculty to present teaching techniques or share outreach initiatives as well. These gatherings allow faculty and students to share ideas, showcase recent breakthroughs, and get feedback on research before it is submitted for publication. In addition to research presentations, conferences also can feature discussion panels, keynote speakers, networking sessions, member's meetings, tours, seminars and specialized training sessions.

Conferences come in all shapes and sizes and go by many names. While "conference" is the most common term, an academic gathering might also be called a workshop, a colloquium, a symposium, a summit, a congress, an annual meeting or a convention. The first few terms often indicate a smaller event, sometimes with a specialized focus or theme. The latter indicate the large annual meeting of an organization, which is broader in focus and larger. For example, the AEJMC Southeast Colloquium is a regional conference that includes sessions from five to six of the association's 33 interest groups, divisions or commissions. Attendance at that meeting typically averages no more than 120. The AEJMC annual conference, in contrast, features programming from all groups and affiliate organizations and can attract 2,500 attendees. Annual conferences typically feature multiple sessions going on at the same time and may include "tracks" (groups of sessions throughout the meeting designed for subsets of attendees; for example, tracks for administrators or teaching faculty).

Conferences typically are organized by academic associations, but they can be hosted by universities, the government or even an independent group of faculty members or professionals with shared interests. In mass communication circles, the broad major associations with national/international conferences include AEJMC, the International Communication Association (ICA) and the National Communication Association (NCA). Other national groups that have a more focused audience include the Broadcast Education Association (BEA), the American Journalism Historians Association (AJHA), the Association for Business Communication (ABC), the American Academy of Advertising (AAA or "the three As") and the Black College Communication Association (BCCA), to name a few. Many of these groups are members of the Council of Communication Associations (CCA; see https://communicationassociations.wordpress.com) and, thus, work collaboratively to serve academics across their memberships.

Still other academic associations are regionally based (for example, the Western Social Science Association, WSSA, which has a mass communication division), are primarily held outside the United States (for example, the International Association for Media and Communication Research, IAMCR), or are designed to serve scholars with connections to communication, regardless of where they're working (for example, the Korean American Communication Association, KACA). Wikipedia has perhaps the most expansive, but not fully exhaustive, list of mass communication-related conferences (see https://en.wikipedia.org/wiki/List_of_communications-related_conferences and feel free to edit and contribute information on conferences you enjoy attending to help others).

FINDING CONFERENCES RIGHT FOR YOU

In a recent survey of 90 AEJMC graduate student members, 74.4 percent of respondents listed faculty mentors and advisors as influencing their choice of which conference to attend. They next cited content/networking opportunities available (64.4 percent of respondents), location (60 percent), cost (56.7 percent), and finally whether peers/classmates planned to attend (38.8 percent) as impacting their conference choices.

Seeking advice from your advisor or other faculty members guiding your research is a great place to start. Seasoned professors have learned from experience what conferences are most receptive to particular topics and approaches. Faculty often have strong preferences, primarily because we invest so much time in the conferences we attend most often. Regardless of whether a conference is hosted by an association, university, institute or an informal consortium, faculty members play central roles throughout the conference beyond presenting their work. They propose panels or sessions, judge research submissions and other competitions, moderate sessions, and provide feedback on the work being presented. In addition to these roles, faculty also are elected or appointed to leadership roles to assist staff (in larger organizations) with running the associations.

Depending on the conference, students also participate in some of these roles. You, too, will become invested in conferences pretty quickly in your academic career. Personal preference on where to attend factors in, of course. And while your professors likely impact decisions starting out, your advisor's conference preferences may not be the place where you feel most at home in the long run. Funding permitting, I encourage you to attend a variety of conferences during graduate school and early in your academic career to get a feel for groups that program meetings that match your interests. Just like people, conferences have different "personalities," and you will find yourself being drawn to a few that fit you best.

Once you've found a few associations or groups you see as a good match, the next step is to explore all the gatherings they offer. For example, AEJMC has two "regional" conferences held early in the year. These allow scholars (often graduate students or early-career faculty members) to refine their research in advance of the April 1 deadline for submission of research to the national conference (held in early August). These regional conferences, which are organized by various divisions and interest groups of AEJMC, are considerably smaller than the annual conference and span just a few days.

I presented my first research paper at the 1994 AEJMC Southeast Colloquium in Charleston, SC, and found the experience much less intimidating than the national conference, where I presented later that year in Atlanta. Although audience size can be just as big or bigger at a regional meeting, many participants are newer to the academy and presenting their first papers, meaning they're all pretty nervous and supportive of others in the same boat. The other attendees are typically faculty accompanying graduate students, and they tend to be supportive and offer constructive feedback delivered in a helpful manner. The other "regional" for AEJMC is the Midwinter Conference, which is younger than the Southeast Colloquium and only requires abstracts for submission, rather than a completed paper.

Under a special rule, papers presented at any AEJMC regional are allowed to be submitted to the AEJMC annual conference, with the understanding that scholars use feedback at these smaller conferences to refine their paper for submission to the annual conference. Similarly, AJHA has a regional conference in Panama City each year (the Southeast Symposium) designed primarily for graduate student papers. Papers presented there also can be submitted to the national AJHA conference. In many other instances, however, papers cannot be submitted if they have been presented elsewhere (see "Acceptance Don'ts" below). If you are attending a regional or smaller conference, be sure to ask the conference organizer what rules govern submission of those papers to the group's national conference.

Because cost is a major factor for graduate students and junior faculty, regional conferences represent an affordable option. Registration costs are lower, because they are often held in less expensive cities. Their short duration cuts down on hotel costs. National conferences, however, are seen as more competitive and more prestigious, so I encourage one national conference a year minimum for emerging scholars, even with the higher price tag.

Most associations offer graduate student perks to help offset the costs, including reduced registration fees, a block of hotel rooms at student rates, cash prizes for top student papers and competitive student travel grants. When you've found a conference to attend, contact the organizer and ask about these types of programs. The Mass Communication and Society Division of AEJMC, for example, has a travel award of up to $1,000 for students attending the midwinter or the national conference. In addition to help from the associations, many departments, schools and colleges allow students to request conference travel funding, and most universities have funding through the graduate school or student government association that can be allocated. Conferences can be a major expense on a student or junior faculty member's salary, but investing in attending—and making the most out of—conferences can have big payoffs for a career long term.

PREPARING FOR THE CONFERENCE: PLANNING YOUR PRESENTATION

Congratulations! You've decided on a conference to attend, submitted a paper and been accepted! You've leapt your first few hurdles and should take time to celebrate your success. The next hurdles, planning out your conference visit and prepping your presentation, are just as important as the ones you've just cleared.

In our zeal to prepare our presentations, we often overlook additional work that is vitally important for getting the most from the conference. One of the first mistakes people at all stages of their academic careers make is booking their travel solely based on the date of their session. This means they may miss out on preconferences, keynotes, networking opportunities and sessions of interest that come earlier or later in the conference. While attending all days of a major conference can be expensive, doing a little research about the optimal days for you will pay off in the long run. For those on the job market (see "The Job Hub"), allowing flexibility for meetings with employers is vitally important. If you're in that position, invest in staying the whole conference to increase your chances to connect.

Now that you have your travel plans, it's time to plan your presentation. Getting your research ready to present is a process that begins with asking questions, much like starting your research project itself. First, ask the person who notified you about your acceptance to clarify the format in which you will present. Presentation formats vary by conference, and the names can be confusing. What's a "Scholar to Scholar" session? In one association, it might be the term for a poster session; another organization might use that term to describe a "speed dating" round of scholars paired to share ideas one-on-one. Other "buzzy" terms you might hear are "Blue Sky Workshop," "Lightening Round," "High Density" and "Round Robin." If you're a newbie, these terms are as clear as mud, so ask what they mean. If you don't get perfect clarity from the person who sent your acceptance, consult with your advisor or others who've attended the conference in the past, scan the conference website or past programs, or contact the association to ensure you are clear about the format, requirements for visuals, time limits and any other specifications.

The most common forms of presentations at conferences are an oral research paper presentation, which can be done in traditional or high-density formats, and a poster presentation. Each takes different preparation, so it's important to fully understand each format before you prep your presentation.

Traditional Research Paper Presentations

Oral research presentations are the most traditional format and still are standard at most conferences. Traditional paper sessions consist of four to five papers presented in a 90-minute or so session with a moderator and a discussant (also sometimes called a respondent). Scholars prepare a 10- to 12-minute talk (confirm your allotted time and stick to it), often accompanied by visuals (PowerPoints are still the most common; check the audiovisual technology available for your session). Audience members can ask questions either directly after each paper or after all have been presented. The moderator typically sets ground rules for questions.

In a few associations or a handful of divisions within larger organizations, it's the norm to read verbatim from a shortened version of the paper. However, at most major U.S. conferences—at least in mass communication and some other disciplines—this practice is rare. Instead, research paper presentations are intended to be short, dynamic lectures that showcase the author's command of the information. When done well, the researcher displays casual mastery of the subject matter as the audience easily follows key points and concepts, even on highly technical topics. Rest assured, however, that it takes meticulous preparation to make a presentation look that effortless. Authors must prepare visuals (and proofread them), make a detailed outline (using bullet points to help you stay on track), and practice to ensure your flow makes sense and you stay well within the time limit. If you use PowerPoints or other visuals, a good rule of thumb is one slide or visual per minute or about a dozen total.

The best paper presentations get the audience hooked right away with an anecdote or visual that explains what sparked the researcher's interest and why the topic matters. The literature review and applicable theory are briefly discussed (no more than two to three slides or a minute or two of the presentation), with the bulk of the time devoted to explaining the research method, results/findings and conclusions. Too many presenters spend so much time on the literature and theory that they barely get to talk about their own research. I've also seen presenters fall into the trap of oversharing limitations and mistakes, which seemingly negates the whole presentation. If people are interested, they'll read the paper, in which the literature and limitations are fully fleshed out.

The moderator's role is to introduce the panel and keep presenters on time. (Make the moderator's job easy by staying under your allotted limit.) A session discussant or respondent gives public feedback on the papers, sometimes as a group, but more often on each paper individually. You may be asked to send your final paper to a moderator and discussant in advance of the conference. Make sure you do so. It's always embarrassing for everyone in the room, but especially the author, to hear the discussant say: "I didn't receive this paper until last night, so I didn't have a chance to read it." Unlike in classes, where grading is between you and the professor, the feedback from the discussant is public. Remember that it is the discussant's job to point out ways to improve the paper. There's no reason to become embarrassed or defensive when you receive constructive criticism; just use this feedback to improve your work. As the discussant (and audience members) make points about your paper, write them down. This not only shows your receptiveness to feedback (even if you aren't going to incorporate it), it helps you remember the key points after the adrenaline rush of the presentation is over.

High-Density Sessions

High-density research paper sessions (also called "lightning rounds" or other terms depending on the organization) often include 10 to 12 research papers presented in a standard session timeframe. The format was created to allow more papers to be presented (thus the term high density) but also to encourage more interaction between the presenter and the audience. Think of high density as a cross between a short traditional oral presentation and a poster, where you interact more informally with people interested in your paper.

Typically, each researcher in a high-density session is given no more than five minutes to present. In some conferences, having a few visuals or slides may be allowed; in others, visuals are not used, but presenters can provide handouts. These mini presentations should be an executive summary with little or no mention of past literature or theoretical contexts. Like traditional paper sessions, a moderator keeps things on track. With a dozen papers, you can imagine how one person going overtime can affect the whole session. Questions typically are not allowed during the presentations.

After the presentations, people break into small groups throughout the room so the author can share more detail and audience members can ask questions. ICA calls these sessions Hybrid High-Density (HHD) sessions, asking researchers to give a brief oral presentation or "teaser" that highlights key questions that the work explores. These ICA sessions then turn into a poster presentation with scholars talking in depth to small groups or one-to-one with audience members. Chuck Lubbers, writing about the high-density format when it was newly launched at AEJMC, explained: "The key is that the individual presentations must be SHORT to allow for individual discussion" after the formal presentations. "This format allows the audience members to hear the detail on those research projects that interest them the most."[2]

The use of discussants or respondents in high-density formats varies. At some conferences, discussants may make a short statement about common themes. In others, the discussant facilitates interaction between scholars and audience members. Moderators or discussants (if both are used) encourage audience members to talk to a few different authors throughout the discussion period. For that reason, Lubbers encourages those presenting in high-density sessions to prepare a handout containing outlines, key findings and relevant data.[3] This handout gives audience members more depth, allows those who don't get a chance to discuss your paper to grab a summary on their way out, and most important, provides your contact information so people can follow up with you. ICA in recent years has encouraged a "digital poster" format for the second part of the

Hybrid High-Density sessions, asking presenters to create an abbreviated poster, slides or infographic to display on their personal electronic devices.

Posters

Poster sessions, sometimes called Scholar to Scholar sessions (AEJMC and NCA) or Interactive Poster sessions (ICA), are held in a large room with multiple bulletin boards that can accommodate dozens of presentations simultaneously. The audience walks through, stopping at papers of interest to talk to researchers standing next to their work. While organizers program the session, there are no moderators. Some conferences use discussants for poster sessions so that authors get feedback regardless of the format in which the accepted papers are presented. Discussants, respondents or, as NCA calls them, "wandering scholars," if used, visit each author during the session and provide feedback, or, at minimum, send comments through e-mail.

Past generations of scholars sometimes attached a stigma to a paper being accepted as a poster, but conference organizers have worked for years to dissuade people of those attitudes. Writing about the growth of the poster format in an article titled "Poster Child? Not Bad" for AEJMC, Jack Rosenberry argued that "no stigma should be attached to poster or high-density sessions. Absolutely no distinction is made in the judging or standards for acceptance based on the presentation venue."[4] NCA also assures its authors that "Scholar to Scholar showcases some of NCA's best-reviewed work."[5]

Papers are slotted in poster sessions not because they are lesser quality but because they don't always group neatly with a themed research session or because a paper topic lends itself to a more visual and interactive format. Many scholars prefer the format because it allows for networking and meaningful discussion with people who are most interested in your work. Rosenberry wrote: "I find it easier—or at least less nerve-wracking—to make a poster showing than to deliver a formal presentation to a room full of colleagues (or to a room devoid of them, which is even worse!) ... I've met colleagues at such sessions who have become close friends and collaborators because of our similar interests."[6] When posters are grouped by division or topic, you interact with people who would have never attended your research paper session but delightedly stumble upon your paper.

In the early days of posters (when technology was limited) many people put up 12 or so PowerPoint slides in order on the board. Now, most everyone does a large poster format (which also can be created and printed in PowerPoint) that they either print at home and bring in a tube to the conference or have printed nearby the conference site. Posters also can be printed on cloth at slightly more cost, but it allows them to be neatly folded into a suitcase or carry-on bag. Above all, look for specifications and requirements on each organization's website before you begin designing.

AEJMC member Sheri Broyles produced a set of tips in an article on the AEJMC website.[7] Her key takeaway? Think big, bold and brief. Use big type that can be read from five feet away, a catchy large headline (rather than the title of the paper), visuals that draw people in and very little text. Most people only skim posters and prefer to engage with the researchers. So be prepared to talk to people about what excited you about the project and what you found. Some people even prepare a brief handout with highlights and their contact information for follow-up discussions. Again, be brief with the literature review, theory and limitations in your poster—people want to know what you did and what you found. The bulk of the poster should focus on your original research, with visuals that help explain your results quickly. Bob Gustafson created a sample layout and formatting tips for the AEJMC website, which can be found at http://www.aejmc.org/home/wp-content/uploads/2013/01/posterboardexample.pdf. ICA also provides tips on posters on its site (https://www.icahdq.org/page/Posters). The association shares photo galleries of all its past conferences, including the poster sessions. Browse the galleries to be inspired as you're looking for creative approaches to your poster (https://www.icahdq.org/page/PastFuture). NCA, on its "Scholar to Scholar FAQs and Tips" page, stresses creativity, writing: "While many will choose to display posters, presenters are invited to use a unique presentation format that best fits the originality of their research and presentation style. These are 'poster sessions' for the 21st century!"[8]

Acceptance Don'ts

Acceptance "dos" are fairly straightforward. On the other hand, over the years, I've collected my share of research paper acceptance "don'ts," which, sadly, I've seen hamper collaboration and career opportunities down the line. I like to think that scholars who've committed these offenses likely haven't been socialized to protocol and didn't know any better. I share this list so that you will know better.

1. Don't submit a paper that you have no intention of presenting. Conference organizers accept papers that will enhance the knowledge in the field. They take great care to organize themed sessions. Those who back out thwart planning and take another person's spot. Everyone understands last-minute emergencies, but

we're all professors and see through fake excuses. I once organized a conference abroad. After I sent out acceptances, scholars wrote me to withdraw their papers because the travel was too expensive. Do your homework before you submit. Make sure you have enough funding and your dates are free. When you submit, you are agreeing to present the paper in person if it is accepted.

2. Don't submit papers to more than one competition or papers that have been presented or published elsewhere. Conference presentations are designed for new, original research. On rare occasions, organization policies allow work presented at its regional conferences to be presented at its national conference (AEJMC and AJHA allow, and even encourage this). If you are unsure of the rules, check with conference organizers. The easiest way to navigate this is to simply submit each paper to one conference at a time. If it's rejected, revise and submit elsewhere. After a paper is accepted, it's fine to submit for publication; however, papers published in journals typically are ineligible for conference presentation.

3. Don't pull a paper scheduled for a "less-than-desirable" session. This is most common for papers scheduled for posters or high-density sessions, although, as noted earlier, these are not second-tier formats. Others withdraw papers scheduled at the very end of a conference. Pulling papers leaves organizers scrambling, takes a spot from someone else, and sends a message that you think you're above certain types of participation or time slots.

4. Don't abandon a paper in a poster session, meaning hanging up your poster and walking away. Also, don't skip the session or conference and have a friend stand by the paper for you. When people stop to chat and your friend admits it's not their work, it reflects poorly on you. These actions defeat the poster session's interactive format. While it is fine to briefly step away from your poster if you have a scheduling conflict, you should spend most of the session with your poster, ready to engage. Perhaps the most egregious behavior I've observed is an author simply taking a copy of the paper (all 30-plus pages of it), thumbtacking it to the board, and leaving. I've seen angry organizers take photos of these boards and heard them discussing the authors who've done this. The impression these actions leave is that the authors do not care enough to engage, believe they are too good for a poster session, or are gaming the system.

5. Above all, don't claim credit for presenting work that you have not. If a coauthor attends and presents, it's totally acceptable to list on a CV; but you get no credit for papers that were not presented. I've seen too many CVs noting a paper was accepted and not presented. If it wasn't presented, leave it out. It doesn't count.

Practice Makes Perfect

No matter what the format of your conference presentation, seek feedback from advisors, colleagues and peers before you present. For traditional paper presentations, practice beforehand in front of an audience, if possible. Many colleges have colloquia opportunities for students and faculty to practice presenting before they attend a conference, so ask your graduate advisor what's offered on your campus. For high-density sessions, practice your summary and have someone look over any visuals or handouts you plan to share. For posters, have someone proofread and give you feedback on the flow and style. No matter how many times you look at something, a fresh set of eyes always will find something you overlooked.

GETTING THE MOST OUT OF THE CONFERENCE

Often, we spend so much time thinking about our presentation, we forget that our session is just one of dozens or even hundreds at a conference. Outside the formal sessions programmed, there are myriad networking and career-enhancing opportunities connected to any academic meeting. Graduate student members in a recent AEJMC survey were asked which features of conferences they found most helpful. Of the 87 respondents, 75.9 percent cited the panels and presentations, 59.8 percent listed networking, and 48.3 percent noted the job hub.

Clearly, presentations are the main reason people attend (to present their work and to see others present), and those on the job market come to get plugged in with those hiring (see "The Job Hub" later in this chapter). But networking, for the most part, takes place outside of those two activities, and finding their opportunities takes preparation. Most groups share their program online in advance of the conference, and attendees who study the program will be well rewarded with a plethora of chances to network. I break these into formally planned organizational sessions and other hidden gems.

Organizational Sessions for Members

If you're new to a conference, especially a large one, look for a "new members'" or "first-time attendees'" session. These typically are held early in the conference, and association leaders will guide you through the opportunities and answer your questions. You'll get the added bonus of meeting others in the same boat as you, and suddenly, a large unfamiliar place feels a little smaller. One quick tip: Many conferences have a ribbon or sticker noting first-time or graduate student attendees. DO NOT TAKE THESE OFF! Sadly, I've seen attendees take these off out of fear of looking like a newbie! You will get a tremendous welcome from all sorts of people who see that ribbon—leaders, association staff, longtime members, potential employers or perhaps a future lifelong friend.

A great place to learn about the organization as a whole is to search the conference program for sessions that bring all members together. These typically are a keynote, presidential address, plenary session or members meeting. You can find these easily on the program because nothing else is scheduled at the same time. I've seen newer members use these times to play tourist, which is a mistake. These sessions are carefully planned to be of broad interest to membership and provide so many learning opportunities about the organization by attending these sessions. Often, major awards are presented, allowing you to see industry leaders and top academics that you might otherwise not get to see. You'll also meet the officers, learn of new initiatives and funding opportunities, and get a feel for how the association is structured. Finally, key decisions are made by members at the business meetings. Association leaders do want all voices heard.

For organizations broken into divisions, interest groups or smaller focused groups, you will find their members meetings on the program. Everyone is welcome to attend these meetings, regardless of whether or not they have joined the group. (You shouldn't vote if you're not a member, of course.) These divisions and groups or organized subject areas (for example, public relations, sports or religion) allow you to make a large organization seem smaller and to connect with people interested in the same things you are. Attending the members meetings gives you a feel for the mission and activities of each group. In recent years, AEJMC also has offered a Division and Interest Group (DIG) Fair, where representatives of the divisions, interest groups and commissions answer questions. Many subgroups have research grants, travel funding and special competitions, and sponsor meetings outside of the conference.

Amanda Bradshaw, who served as head of the Graduate Student Interest Group (GSIG) of AEJMC in 2019–2020, volunteered for a leadership role in GSIG as a second-year doctoral student. "One of the best strategies ... is to dive right in and get involved in smaller subcommittees, divisions, or interest groups to form strong interpersonal relationships," she wrote.[9] She soon was tapped by the president of AEJMC to work on an ad-hoc committee to help the association better assist graduate student researchers. As the head of GSIG, she learned to manage paper submissions and assign reviewers, to find discussants and moderators, and to create panel topics related to teaching, research and service. As such, she's seen "the process from the inside out. This has better equipped me to prepare my own research submissions to conferences and has, frankly, encouraged me to be even more critical of my own academic scholarship. Likewise, the connections that I have formed with other graduate students and faculty members have provided immeasurable value."[10]

The Hidden Gems

Many of the best networking opportunities are hiding in plain sight on the program, but the lingo is confusing to newcomers. This section is designed to decode some of those terms so you can find opportunities that are right for you.

The Exhibit Hall. No, it's not a stuffy museum with priceless artifacts. It's just a place where companies, programs and groups have set up tables to connect you with things that will help you do your job. Think book publishers, other associations, software vendors, foundations and groups that support journalists and educators. People at the tables want to talk to you and want to help you. The book publishers, for example, want you to buy their books, adopt books for your classes or pitch manuscripts to them (you might get a book deal out of stopping by). Bonus: Most are giving away free stuff or at least have candy on their tables. Another bonus: You'll run into other attendees interested in the same things you are and strike up conversations. Yet another bonus: Exhibit halls typically are where associations host their refreshment breaks (more free stuff). As a grad student, my "meals" were the cookies and popcorn in the AEJMC Exhibit Hall.

Receptions and Socials. Look for opportunities designed solely for networking. These include conference-wide socials or receptions but also can include group and institutional events. Again, free food, and at some, free drinks! (Are you sensing a trend?) If you've gone to a divisional members meeting, it often is followed by the group's social. In most cases, all who attend meetings are welcome to attend socials as long as preregistration wasn't required. If in doubt, just ask. No one will be offended, and groups love to host prospective members. You'll also find socials listed in the program hosted by universities or other organizations. While these are designed to be gathering places for alumni and faculty, most are widely open to friends as well. Friends are defined as anyone who could one day study, work or collaborate with the university, which is, really, any of us. Honestly, if a social is in the program, organizers are totally fine with new members attending. If the event is private, it won't be in the program (or listed as "by invitation only"). Finally, many divisions or affiliated groups offer luncheons or other meals, and you'll find these listed in the conference program. For the most part, these require advanced ticketing, as organizers need counts to order the food and ticket sale proceeds to help offset the costs. These are wonderful opportunities for people to connect with people, and often they are listed on the conference registration form. If you find something that looks interesting and you can afford the ticket, I encourage you to attend.

Out-of-Convention Sessions. Great training, information and networking opportunities can be found during pre- and postconference sessions as well as off-site tours. These sessions, which can range from two hours to all day, tend to be focused on a particular topic or industry and include a limited number of participants, allowing you to connect more deeply with people who share your interests. Off sites, preconferences and postconferences are usually offered for a minimal charge and require preregistration. Check the conference registration page and the program to see what sessions are available and plan accordingly. If you find something of interest to you, go to the group's web page (or e-mail the group's head) and find out more. These trainings and off-site visits are advertised in the members newsletters and on the division's website.

THE JOB HUB

If you are on the job market, planning for a conference takes on a whole new meaning. In addition to having to organize your presentations, sessions and events, you have to juggle a kind of speed dating experience where you're looking for potential matches with colleges and universities. Most major annual conferences have some type of service that matches those looking to hire with graduate students and others entering the job market. This is an excellent opportunity for both sides to explore whether the student would like to become a formal candidate for the position.

For example, in the AEJMC Job Hub, employers provide information about current or anticipated job openings in the coming academic year. Those on the market upload their vita, browse what's available, who will be at the conference, and request meetings with those who have open positions of interest. Potential employers review your materials and then let you know if they are available to sit down and talk with you during the conference. Most of these meetings are informal, lasting roughly 20 minutes, and should be a two-way conversation. Job candidates should do a little research on the program before the meeting, so they can ask questions about teaching load, research expectations, leadership, direction and so on. This book contains an entire chapter on the job hunt, but I wanted to note the key role that conference job match services can play. These informal chats at conferences are a great way for both the candidate and the university to get a feel for each other's strengths.

CONFERENCE PROTOCOL

Whether or not you are actively on the job market, once you enter academia, you're always on the job market—even if you don't know it. The connections and the impressions we make at conferences can help propel us into new opportunities that we never imagined, regardless of where we are in our careers. For me, I was recruited into a department chair's job at the University of Alabama based on connections I made at AEJMC conferences over the years. Later, my interactions with people at the University of Kentucky (UK) through SEC athletic conference programs were a key factor in my interest in the dean's job at UK. In each case, I didn't realize I was looking until the opportunity came calling.

For all the thousands of people that attend some of our largest conferences, it's amazing how many people you will run into again and again throughout the world and throughout your career. Good impressions last; bad impressions last even longer. This section is designed to help graduate students and early-career faculty attending academic conferences make good impressions that last and avoid bad ones.

Dos and Don'ts for Conference Attendees

- DO: Ask about attire. Some conferences are pretty informal, with attendees in jeans. At others, it's rare someone is not wearing a suit. If you are presenting, I always recommend business casual, at minimum.
- DON'T: Worry if you're caught in the elevator wearing something super casual as you head out to sightsee. Just take your nametag off and people will think nothing of it.
- DO: Jot down questions during others' presentations so you're ready with questions at the end. It's always so uncomfortable for presenters and the audience alike when no one has questions. Scholars want to engage with the audience. Help them out.
- DON'T: Ask a "question" that really is just a platform to talk about your own research. I saw a "question" go on for more nearly ten minutes once, and I just kept praying for the moderator to step in.
- DO: Be courteous with everyone at the conference, even if you disagree with the points a person has made in a presentation. Raise alternate viewpoints in a constructive way.
- DON'T: Provoke presenters because you they disagree with them or want to show off your knowledge.
- DO: Be present as much as possible in the sessions you're attending. Think of how you would like your audience to act when you're presenting, and act that way when you are in the audience.

- DON'T: Sit in a presentation totally focused on your phone, tablet or computer, or worse yet, talk to friends throughout a session. If you're not going to engage, you can check your e-mail or visit in the lobby.
- DO: Network, Network, Network. Take time to connect with a variety of people in various settings throughout the conference. You may just find a future coauthor or, even better, someone from outside your institution who can mentor you. I've found both at conferences in my career—and have formed some great friendships to boot.
- DON'T: Treat the conference like a vacation, or worse, spring break at Daytona. I've seen people get sloppy drunk (and loud) at receptions or socials. Knowing your limits is not just for driving. Although it's fine to kick back with friends, conference events are professional settings, even if the alcohol is free.

CONCLUSION

Conference organizers want everyone to get something out of the conference, be comfortable and be engaged. We want people to be themselves and have fun. Knowing the norms of each particular organization or of conference behavior in general can help all involved achieve their goals. Just remember, at academic conferences, you are presenting yourself as much as you're presenting your research.

Academic conferences are not just something you can coast into or haphazardly approach. To get the most out of them takes careful preparation and investment of time. But the payoffs can be huge. You absolutely can change your career trajectory through connections and impressions made at conferences. I know that firsthand. And when I was AEJMC president at "my" conference (2018, Washington, D.C.), one of the most fun experiences I had was introducing myself to first-time graduate student attendees. When they saw my purple "President" name tag ribbon, I saw their eyes light up. One even gave out a little gasp. At that moment, I thought of my fangirl moment with Steve Chaffee and the "club" that we were all in. We're delighted that you're part of the club now, too. Just wait for the point in your career when a graduate student gapes when meeting you at an academic conference. Trust me, it will happen.

NOTES

[1] Amy M. Buddie, "Academic Conferences 101: What They Are, Why Go, How to Present and How To Pay For It All," American Psychological Association. Accessed January 21, 2020. https://www.apa.org/ed/precollege/psn/2016/09/academic-conferences.

2. Chuck Lubbers, "High Density Sessions," AEJMC. Accessed January 29, 2020. http://www.aejmc.org/home/2013/01/high-density-sessions/.
3. Lubbers, "High Density Sessions."
4. Jack Rosenberry, "Poster Child, Not Bad," AEJMC. Accessed January 21, 2020. http://www.aejmc.org/home/2013/01/poster-child-not-bad/.
5. National Communication Association, "Scholar to Scholar FAQS and Tips," Accessed February 2, 2020. https://www.natcom.org/convention-events/convention-resources/convention-resource-library/scholar-scholar-faqs-and-tips.
6. Rosenberry, "Poster Child, Not Bad."
7. Sheri Broyles, "About Poster Sessions," AEJMC. Accessed December 12, 2019. http://www.aejmc.org/home/2013/01/about-poster-sessions/.
8. NCA, "Scholar to Scholar FAQs and Tips." Accessed March 23, 2020. https://www.natcom.org/convention-events/convention-resources/convention-resource-library/scholar-scholar-faqs-and-tips.
9. Amanda Bradshaw (Head, GSIG), e-mail to the author, February 2, 2020.
10. Bradshaw, e-mail to the author.

7

Publishing as a Graduate Student

Denise Sevick Bortree, Penn State University, and
Richard D. Waters, University of San Francisco

In today's competitive academic job market, doctoral students find that they need to begin their publication track record during graduate school. Publishing book chapters and peer-reviewed journal articles as a graduate student can be a way to set yourself apart from other job candidates and offers many other benefits. At first, publishing may seem daunting or even impossible. How can you make the jump from writing papers for class to submitting journal manuscripts? The publication process typically begins with class papers, which then become conference papers, eventually turned into publications. Working with peers and reaching out to trusted mentors can help you succeed. In this chapter, we walk you through the advantages of publishing now, answer graduate student questions and outline the process itself.

WHY PUBLISH DURING GRAD SCHOOL?

As a graduate student, you are learning to balance classwork with your teaching or research assistantship, and so the expectation to begin publishing during graduate school may be overwhelming. Despite what you may think, you have the time and knowledge you need to begin moving toward publishing. Publishing has many benefits, including focusing your research interests, honing your research skills and improving your chances of landing a good job. In the next sections we will talk about many of these benefits.

Building Knowledge Areas

Through publishing, you can explore your research passion and begin to develop a research agenda as you write and conduct research related to your dissertation or thesis topic. This research track record can give a job candidate an advantage, and it can also help build a solid foundation of research that new faculty members can build on as they navigate the tenure track years. A best practice for graduate research productivity is to conduct one or two other related studies in the broad area of your dissertation or thesis topic. You may consider starting with class papers and building to conference papers. This will improve your understanding of the literature in the field, and you can draw on findings from your other studies as you write your dissertation or thesis. This exploration will also provide insight into the academic appetite for the topic. As you learn more about your specific communications discipline, you will learn what was been covered, by whom and when, along with discovering gaps in the literature. These gaps create a space for your scholarship, both now and in the future. Feedback from reviewers may help you identify key issues with your approach to the topic, and that can help drive your future projects.

Learning to Balance Research with Other Obligations

Graduate school is a busy time. Classes can be demanding, especially paired with assistantships, teaching and other duties. Balancing classwork and teaching preparation can be difficult. However, learning this balance sets the foundation for life on the tenure track. The earlier that you learn to balance multiple academic responsibilities, the more successful your academic experience will be. Carving out a few hours per week to conduct your own research and move it to the publication stage can be very rewarding.

Learning to Collaborate

Graduate students and faculty who have similar research interests often collaborate on projects and coauthored publications. Learning strategies for being a good research collaborator can lead to more invitations to collaborate on projects. Later in this chapter, we'll outline best practices for working with a team of researchers to develop and implement a research project.

Gaining Experience with the Peer Review Process

In the graduate school classroom, completing a research project often means writing a final paper, reporting the results of a research study and maybe presenting the findings to fellow classmates and your instructor. But, the larger goal in academia is to publish the research findings so others can learn from them and build on them. This includes additional steps such as submitting the paper to a conference (and presenting it) and submitting the paper for consideration as a book chapter or peer-reviewed journal article. Experience with this process, including how to respond to revise and resubmit decisions, can help a researcher be more successful with their manuscript submissions.

PUBLISHING QUESTIONS FROM GRADUATE STUDENTS

We asked a group of graduate students for their questions about publishing. Below are their questions and the answer we would give our graduate students. Note that some of these responses are program-dependent, so we recommend checking with your advisor or program director for their answers to these questions.

How Early in Graduate School Should Students Start Thinking About Publishing?

It's never too early to start working on research in graduate school, but chances that your first paper will find its way to the pages of a peer-reviewed journal are slim (although it does happen). However, in order to have publications on your vitae during your academic job search (typically at the beginning of your fourth year), you should probably be thinking about starting the publishing process during your second year. We will cover this in greater depth in another answer below.

Should I Involve My Advisor in the Publication Process?

That depends on you, your advisor and your project. Students are not required to include their advisor in the publication process if this person was not part of the project. However, during your early years in a graduate program, your advisor can help you develop research ideas, identify the best outlets for research and tackle revisions. As you become more experienced with the publication process, you will be able to handle this on your own. But never feel like you cannot solicit feedback on a manuscript from your advisor. Chances are they will be willing to offer guidance on any work that you feel has potential for publication. You should feel free to work with other faculty as well. If you developed a class paper that has potential for a conference or journal submission, consider contacting the instructor of the course to get more feedback and guidance. Faculty can also guide you on where to submit a manuscript.

Should I Seek a Faculty Member to Partner With?

Early in your graduate program, consider developing research collaborations with experienced faculty, which can help you learn more about navigating a project. One way to do this is to ask faculty members with similar research interests if they need help on any of their projects. You may find that they would welcome your help. Another approach is to develop a few research ideas based on your reading of the literature or on a class paper topic that you have completed, and solicit faculty members' feedback, inquiring about a possible collaboration. If they do not have time, they will likely direct you to a colleague that may be interested. Either way, you are likely to receive good suggestions for how to implement the project. Another collaboration opportunity is through grant funding. Faculty who have funding often look for graduate students to work on projects with them. It never hurts to politely ask about opportunities.

Should I Work on a Team and/or Collaborate on Research Projects during Graduate School?

Collaborative research can come with many benefits. Working with a team of other researchers can help spark ideas that a single researcher might not produce; it also provides more time for tedious or time-consuming tasks, like coding or transcribing interviews. Members bring their own strengths, such as data analysis or writing literature reviews, and together they can produce a better product. Additionally, if you work with others with similar interests but different experiences or different knowledge, you will learn skills and information that you can take to future projects.

Some graduate programs offer lab groups or research groups focused on a single academic area. This can be a good way to experience your first collaborative project. For example, in the Bellisario College of Communications at Penn State, students choose from a wide range of research groups that focus on media effects, advertising, public relations, health communications or other topics. Students in the groups work together to choose research ideas and implement research studies, while being guided by experienced faculty members.

Not all collaborations are productive, positive experiences, however. Decision-making can be challenging if all members are not on the same page. And if a key member of the group loses interest or does not have enough time, the project can languish and possibly never be completed.

Avoid these pitfalls by choosing collaborations wisely. Learn how to say "no" when asked to work on a project that sounds interesting, but may not be your best interest. Just because collaborations are available doesn't mean that they must be accepted. This valuable lesson will also help you on the tenure track. Projects that sound compelling—a theoretical perspective that is close to one's own research agenda, for example—come up all the time when connections with colleagues are strong. At the end of the day, no one has the time to do it all. Whether a seasoned full professor or a new graduate student, everyone needs to learn to say "no" when the proverbial research plate is too full or when they simply need more time for their work–life balance. This is not to discourage you from collaboration, but help you to identify which projects are worth your time at this stage in your career.

How Do You Decide Authorship Order for a Multiauthored Publication?

Author order on a publication can be a sensitive subject, and it's best to address it toward the beginning of a project. Typically, the person who contributes the most to the work and the idea formation is given first authorship, and others are listed in order of their contribution. However, for some projects the originality of the contribution may be considered more valuable than the number of hours contributed. In this case, the order of authorship might look different.

The best way to manage authorship is to clearly identify order in its development phase. The first author takes leadership of the project, managing the process, and makes a significant contribution to the overall work. That person should be determined early and should agree to these responsibilities. The group should then decide each team member's tasks and assign authorship based on the workload. This will eliminate uncomfortable conversations at the end of the project, as team members try to determine who contributed the most (and in what order).

Should I Focus Only on My Dissertation or Thesis Topic (or Closely Related Topics) for Any Publications during Graduate School?

Publishing on your dissertation or thesis topic is an excellent idea, and we would encourage you to make that a priority. However, realistically, many of your early research projects will come from classes that you take during your program, which may address topics outside of your dissertation or thesis focus. That's not a problem. You should try to publish these projects, as well. That said, be sure to make a fair assessment of a class paper's publication potential before investing time on it. A faculty member may be able to help you with this. Research conducted by your lab or research group may not fit with your dissertation or thesis topic. This additional scholarship can give you exposure to other research ideas, theories and methods. And, gaining experience with the publication process can be useful.

How Can I Start and Maintain a Stream of Research While in Graduate School?

As you think about a research agenda or stream of research, we would suggest that you think in general topic areas. You have the latitude to explore topics using a variety of theories and methods. With your research area defined broadly, you can focus your class papers and collaborative projects, looking at the topic from many perspectives. We (the authors of this book chapter) focused on nonprofit communication during graduate school (and the tenure track), which allowed us to take a look at a variety of topics, including donor relations, volunteer communication, social media communication by nonprofits and environmental advocacy.

As your research agenda develops and connects to other related topics and theoretical perspectives, think about crafting data collection instruments that gather data for multiple projects. You should not sacrifice the quality of your research questions in an individual project in favor of securing multiple perspectives on a particular topic, but there are ways to segment data to represent different theoretical perspectives. Whether this is through having different sections on surveys that ask unrelated questions or having content analysis questions that ask coders to review material from new perspectives, it is possible to conceive a research project and design an instrument that allows you to maximize the potential for collecting data. When you're dedicating time to design and carry out a project well, figuring out a way to add a few more questions or observations to look for can lead to a second (or third) paper, ultimately strengthening your research agenda.

As you move onto the tenure track (for those who choose to do so) you will be able to narrow your focus to specific theories and more specialized applications. But, for graduate school, avoid utilizing too narrow of a focus.

Can I Send a Conference Paper to a Journal? How Are Conference Papers and Journal Articles Different?

The short answer is "yes" you can submit a conference paper to a journal. However, a good practice is to incorporate feedback from the conference reviewers into a stronger version of the paper. One place to start with your editing is to strengthen your arguments for the study and provide a solid rationale for the method, as well as in the paper's conclusions. You might have a trusted faculty member read your conference paper to provide additional suggestions about how to prepare it for a journal.

In general, journal submissions are accepted at a lower rate than conference papers. That means getting into a journal is much more competitive. As a result, the quality of work published in a journal tends to be higher than at a conference, meaning that journal reviewers expect more than those reviewing manuscripts for a conference. Chances are, you will need to make some revisions to your conference paper before submitting it to a journal.

Should Everyone Publish in Graduate School?

Graduate students should try to publish during graduate school. The purpose of graduate school is to prepare you to contribute to the larger conversation in your academic field, and that happens in the field's journals. By publishing, you are contributing the knowledge you gained through your research studies. However, there might be cases where it does not make sense. For example, if a student plans to work in the professional world after graduate school, they might not need to demonstrate their ability to publish. The same is true for someone who plans to take a teaching (non-tenure-line) position. However, most schools, even teaching-focused schools, have some research expectations for their tenure-line faculty, so completing a research project and publishing it would be helpful for applicants on the job market.

What's the Right Balance between Classroom Papers/Work and Outside Projects?

Your classwork is a priority in graduate school, but you need to also work on your own research studies. Most students try to get one to two conference papers submitted per year (and some do more like four to five). Dr. Michail Vafeiadis (assistant professor, Auburn University) reflected, "One piece of advice that I received as a doctoral student is that you need to juggle approximately five projects every semester, but which are in different stages. For example, you might want to work on two new projects, while working on an R&R [revise and resubmit], or collecting data for another paper." We strongly support Dr. Vafeiadis' suggestion that you work on multiple papers at a time. As you complete class papers, revise and submit them to conferences. After presenting your conference papers, revise and submit them to journals.

Is It Better to Have More Journal Articles or to Have Articles in Better Journals?

This is a tricky question to answer because the number of publications is important, but so is the quality of the journals in which they are published. Higher quality research typically takes more time (and maybe more resources), so sometimes quality and quantity are inverse. When someone refers to "better" journals they typically mean journals with a lower acceptance (percentage of submitted manuscripts accepted) or with a higher impact factor (average number of citations made to articles in a journal). These are important indicators of quality and influence of a journal, and you should consider them when you submit your work. However, they do not always tell you where the most important conversations are happening for your research topic. The best strategy for successful publishing is to identify journals that publish articles highly related to your research focus. By publishing your research in those journals, you'll be contributing to the broader academic conversation. This makes your work more relevant and useful to the field. So, while quality and quantity are important, try to focus most on your overall contribution to the conversation in your field. If you maintain a stream of research, as suggested in other sections of this chapter, conference papers will become journal publications, and that will help you reach a good quantity of publications. Shoot for both quality and quantity, but most importantly, focus on the relevance of your work to the journal. Lastly, never pay to publish an article. If a journal editor is asking for sums of money, it is likely a scam.

How Do I Appropriately Ask for and Secure Funding for Ongoing Research?

Research funding can open up doors for graduate students by providing money to pay participants in surveys and experiments or pay interview subjects. Research money can also be used to travel or buy equipment (computers, laptops, recorder, camera) needed to collect data. And, sometimes research funding is used to pay the researcher's salary or other expenses. But, accessing this funding can be difficult. Some programs offer summer money to their graduate students. This could be a few thousand dollars to help students with living expenses while they work on research. Other programs may offer small grants that require an application process and a detailed description of the research to be conducted. Check with your program to see what is available for you.

Other organizations offer funding for graduate student research, mostly by supporting faculty member researchers who include students in their work. For example, government entities such as the National Science

Foundation or the National Institutes of Health fund research grants that can include graduate student assistants. Smaller grants are available through communication centers, such as the Arthur W. Page Center at Penn State University or through communication associations such as AEJMC or the National Communication Association.

How Do I Time My Publications for the Job Market?

The publication process can take a long time, from the study conceptualization to the appearance of the final journal article in print (sometimes up to two years or more). Given that the academic hiring process occurs nearly a year before a position begins, you need to start early in your graduate program to have publications on your vitae during the application process. If you can, submit to journals by the end of your second year of a four-year doctoral program. Some publications will take a year or less, and that means you will have a publication in your third year of the program. Some journals will take longer. So, if your goal is to have a publication on your vitae by the fall of your fourth year, you may want to start thinking about publishing in your second year. Book chapters, on the other hand, can be more quickly accepted, depending on the book editor. This is also a good option for adding publications to your vitae before hitting the job market.

What Are Various Types of Institutions Looking for in Terms of Research Production?

Universities vary in their research and teaching expectations. Schools that are designated by the Carnegie Classification of Institutions of Higher Education as Research I have the highest research expectations. Other universities and colleges may expect less research productivity but higher teaching quality and frequency. Schools with a higher research expectation will be looking for job candidates with more research output during graduate school. Keep this in mind as you decide where you might want to work in the future and plan your focus in graduate school accordingly.

STAGES OF PUBLISHING IN JOURNALS

Academics are always in at least one of the stages of publishing. Though the school calendar may dictate that some periods of the year are more active than others in regard to researching, writing and publishing, this component of an academic's career never ends. In the question and answer section of the chapter, we introduced taking class and conference papers to journals, but we wanted to use this step-by-step process to highlight the different stages of the publishing process and issues you might face during each stage.

Stage 1: Setting Up the Research Project

As discussed earlier, you likely have several class papers or conference papers that you have worked on by yourself or in a collaborative effort with a faculty advisor, mentor or a fellow student. We wanted to reiterate the value of the interpersonal network when it comes to devising research projects. Your research agenda will grow considerably when you're able to talk to these individuals, helping you gain additional insights on new theoretical perspectives, data collection processes and other aspects. For example, during a graduate class at the University of Florida, we collected data mapping the continuum of organizational relationships, resulting in multiple journal articles that compared relationship types, as well as how relationships were evaluated differently based on demographic variables.

Stage 2: Setting Up the Structure of Your Manuscript

Whether you are preparing your class paper for a conference or a journal, the structure of the manuscript will look very similar in its layout. Research papers generally consist of an introduction, literature review, method section, results/findings, discussion and a conclusion. While there are several different ways to write your manuscript, we have found success in taking this approach with each of the sections. The introduction addresses current trends, background statistics or current events to introduce the focal topic of the article, and it always ends with a clear purpose statement that highlights what your research is going to address. Next, the literature review provides a survey of recent and historical scholarly works and relevant industry publications that help lead into your research questions. Avoid lumping your research questions or hypotheses all together at the end of the section. Depending on the type of research conducted, you may also have sections for the historical background and theoretical framework.

The method section is crucial to all papers (other than those that use an integrated historical approach). Be as detailed as possible, for the method section is to be as detailed as possible, documenting every step that you went through as the researcher to collect the data for the project. Your colleagues should be able to read your method section and be able to carry out your research project exactly as you did if they had the same resources and access to data sources that you did. I generally tell my graduate student advisees to err on the side of providing too many details for transparency sake. This definitely includes providing information about the questions asked in an interview, scales used on a survey, codebook for a content analysis, or a textual analysis sample, but it also includes more specific details, such as the location and incentives offered for focus group participation, the criteria used to separate participants into experiment groups, and the software and processes used for recording and transcribing interviews. The more detailed you are in the method section, the fewer objections you're likely to have from reviewers once you submit the manuscript to a journal.

The method section should only talk about the research process, including hypotheses and research questions, information about the methodology, including how data was collected and if any statistical pre-tests were used to determine if scales were reliable, and a description of the sample. Every once in a while, we see manuscripts list the demographic profile of their participants in the method section or findings identified from a text. But these are actually part of the next section. The results/findings section should be where you present all of the data that has been collected and analyzed, answering the research questions or hypotheses with statistical data, participants' quotations, tables, charts, themes identified and other pieces of evidence you have collected, according to the methodology guiding the study. Separate your interpretation from the actual presentation findings, offering a straightforward reporting of evidence in a well-organized structure that matches the method section. If you add any visuals like a table or figure, include that as an appendix rather than inserting the entire visual into the text of the manuscript.

The discussion section is where you interpret those findings. Start by summarizing the findings in one short paragraph that explains the statistical findings or reiterates the key themes identified in qualitative approaches. This is particularly helpful with using research articles in teaching classes when students may not understand the statistical tests at all. Then circle back to the literature review, using secondary research to support your interpretations of the findings. Highlight the aspects that confirm our existing knowledge and note those findings that contradict previous research, demonstrating how your research addresses gaps in the literature. It may be helpful to think about the discussion in terms of theoretical contributions and practical application. That way you're making your research more accessible and meaningful to a larger audience.

Every research paper ends with a conclusion, which is often not given the attention that it deserves. The conclusion should always have a limitations section where you acknowledge weaknesses in your research design. There's no such thing as the perfect research project, as there are always ways to expand the collection of data or the analysis techniques that we simply didn't think about or have the ability to do. It's important to acknowledge those weaknesses because readers are going to have questions about your research decisions. You need to defend those choices while acknowledging that there are other approaches that could have been taken. The conclusion also needs to have a future research section that highlights new possible avenues of inquiry based on the findings. It should not be viewed as a section where you simply suggest the opposite philosophical approach to research than what was presented in the current study (e.g., if you did a survey, suggest that a qualitative inquiry would help provide details not revealed by the statistical analysis). Instead, take time to explore what new research ideas have emerged from your study, and you'll be able to expand your own research agenda while also encouraging other scholars to venture down these new research streams.

Stage 3: Choosing a Journal for Your Manuscript

It is worth the time to think carefully about where you submit an article. A manuscript should only be under review at one journal. Do not submit the same work to more than one journal outlet. As far as what journal, there has been a proliferation in traditional and online academic journals as research interests and agendas have become more interdisciplinary. Journals are regularly evaluated for their impact and prestige based on multiple performance measures, including the number of articles accepted and/or rejected each year, the average number of citations per article, the number of citations received from other "top journals," the number of downloads per article and other index-specific measures. Internationally, several countries have their own designated lists of top-tier journals based on their own criteria. Ultimately, rankings of journals do matter when your curriculum vitae is under review for tenure, but the ranking isn't the only factor to consider when submitting a manuscript.

The first item that should be considered is whether a research project's focus is a strong fit with past topics and methods that the journal has included. A discipline may have multiple journals dedicated to publishing its work, but different journals have emerged as being better outlets for certain types of work. Public relations, for example, has *Journal of Public Relations Research*, *Public Relations Review* and *Public Relations Inquiry*. All three journals serve the same academic community, but the journals have evolved to have different specialties. *Journal of Public Relations Research* tends to focus more on quantitative works that develop and advance theory. *Public Relations Review* has theory in its works, but it is much more focused on the practical, day-to-day application of public relations concepts. *Public Relations Inquiry*, on the other hand, is much more welcoming to qualitative and critical/cultural perspectives. Knowing the differences in your discipline's journals will help significantly in determining fit of a particular journal.

In addition to reviewing your discipline's major journals, you should also be on the lookout for special publishing opportunities. Journals regularly publish special issues that feature issues of research that are narrowly focused on a particular topic or event, theoretical perspective or method in a discipline. Given the potential for highlighting new topics or perspectives, special issues are good opportunities for graduate students to be able to submit their work when their research agendas might not normally fit the journal's historical interests. Subscribing to multiple associations' listservs and their social media outreach help academics stay connected to the many special publishing opportunities.

Stage 4: Preparing the Manuscript for Submission

After you've decided on which journal to submit to, you'll need to explore its submission process. While each journal will have its own submission guidelines, the transition to processing manuscripts online has resulted in several similarities. You should anticipate preparing multiple files for submitting your work, including a cover letter, a title page, a blinded manuscript that contains the research text and reference list, an abstract separate from the manuscript text, and separate files for any tables or figures that accompany the text. The cover letter should highlight key findings, discuss the work's importance and state any unique situations pertaining to the work, including funding sources, potential conflicts of interest and whether the research was carried out under the auspices of any agency or organization. You should also state that your manuscript is not under submission elsewhere, nor has it been previously published.

The title page lists the name of the manuscript and the full names and titles of authors in the order determined by the researchers. The title page should also list the initial date of submission to the journal and specify a subhead used on the blinded manuscript in case there are any issues with the computer-automated merging of files for the review process. The manuscript should be blinded so that authors are not identified anywhere in the text (which is grounds for disqualification). If the authors are citing their own previous research, it is fine to cite that work as long as first-person pronouns (e.g., I, my, we, our) are not used in reference to that research. Finally, any tables or figures should be included as a separate file so that reviewers can see the material as it pertains to the text. You shouldn't try to place this material in the text of the manuscript because the layout and design process will ultimately dictate where it will go; however, you should add a placeholder indicating "Table One

Goes Here" or "Figure One Goes Before Research Questions" to provide context for those involved in the design stage.

Journal Guidelines. Seasoned academics and new graduate students should equally abide by journal policies when submitting their work initially. A 5,000-word or a 20-page limit is a serious limit for journal articles. Going over these limits egregiously could result in an immediate desk rejection by the editor and prevent the work from ever being seen by that journal's reviewers. It is often difficult to edit research papers down to journal length when they stem from dissertations, theses, or even course papers. But it is needed to maximize the publication potential for your work.

Ultimately, disciplines may use different citation styles for their journals as well. Even though the American Psychological Association (APA) is most often used by social sciences, there are journals even within our own field that use other styles, including Modern Language Association (MLA) or Chicago/Turabian style. Whether a journal uses in-text citations, footnotes/endnotes and other style-specific notations, it is important to review journal guidelines and edit your manuscript appropriately. It is worth the time to reformat. Submitting a manuscript in a wrong style may result in an immediate rejection for not following the journal's guidelines.

Stage 5: Responding to Editors' and Reviewers' Critiques

Once the manuscript and its corresponding files have been submitted to a journal electronically, the editor then seeks out reviewers who have expertise in the submission's topic and/or research method. Often, authors will be asked to submit specific keywords that connect to the research to aid in the reviewer selection process. Manuscripts are typically sent out to three reviewers, who are asked to critically review the work within six weeks. During that time, the reviewers read the manuscript and prepare detailed notes for the editor and the authors of the manuscript. If you haven't heard anything after six weeks, you can politely contact the editor of the journal and ask for a status update.

Their notes are usually accompanied with a recommendation for the editor to either "Accept As Is," "Accept With Minor Revisions," "Revise/Resubmit" or "Reject" the manuscript. Manuscripts usually only receive the "accept as is" recommendation after it has been through the review process, and accepting a manuscript with minor revisions is rare with the initial submission.

You should be excited if you get a "revise and resubmit," in which an author is asked to revise a manuscript and resubmit it, incorporating the reviewers' critiques. This can be daunting at times given that the critiques from the three reviewers may be very different and possibly contradicting. Read the reviewers' comments and see which suggestions are easy to implement and which the authors are able to do. You may disagree with some of the suggestions, which may be out of the scope of the paper or require collecting additional data. See if they appear across reviews and then consult your advisor or a faculty member on how to approach the revision. As the author, you have to determine what you are and are not willing to do. Despite social media memes about the infamous Reviewer #2, reviewers are not out to ruin manuscripts, gain citations for themselves or squash new ideas. The goal of the reviewing process is to strengthen manuscripts and research so that the discipline overall is improved through higher quality research. Good editors will help interpret the tone and tenor of reviews that may have strong wording. It is rarely done with malicious intent, but some reviewers may have pet peeves or specific flaws that they have seem repeatedly in manuscripts that they may critique harshly.

When asked for the best advice she has been given about revise and resubmits, Carlina DiRusso (graduate student, Penn State) said, "Don't be afraid to get the editor involved if the reviewers are 'wrong' (and you have a valid argument and you can reason why they are wrong), yet they are still not cooperating with you. A good editor should mediate between reviewers and submitters as needed." If you decide to revise and resubmit a manuscript, keep in mind that you will be asked to prepare a resubmission cover letter that documents the changes that have been made. Requested revisions outside of what you can feasibly do can be placed in the limitations and future research section. Your overall letter should be clear and concise—written in a manner that is respectful of the reviewers' time and expertise. Keep in mind the same reviewers will be reading the resubmission and your letter. They decide whether the manuscript will receive the prized acceptance decision. There are times when a revise and resubmit decision is given to a manuscript, but the authors should walk away from that journal instead. Reviewers may simply ask for too much additional work, or perhaps authors aren't sure how to manage within the word or page limits they have been given. Authors certainly can ask the editors if there is any leniency in the revision, but tread carefully and with politeness and respect. Given the multitude of journals that are out there, it may be time to turn to another journal.

Stage 6: Working with a Rejected Manuscript

First off, if you receive a rejection, don't get too upset over the decision. Academia is full of rejections. Take a day and then think about your next potential outlet. Do not ignore the feedback from the original journal, editor and its reviewers. That feedback should be incorporated into strengthening the manuscript for submission to another journal, especially the critiques that can easily be done. Scholars that resubmit the exact same files for submission at Journal A to Journal B without incorporating any changes run the risk of having the same reviewers seeing the manuscript again. Given the role that topic, theory and method keywords are used to determine which journal reviewers are going to be selected to review a manuscript, the same person might be asked to review research that is submitted to different outlets. The odds become even greater when you submit research to more prestigious journals that rely on a smaller pool of reviewers who are full or associate professors. We have received the exact same manuscript from multiple journals several times, and one particular manuscript was submitted in the exact same condition on three separate occasions after it was rejected from previous journals. Each round of reviews offers suggestions for improving your manuscript, and authors should plan to incorporate these changes to the best of their abilities.

The reviewers' feedback isn't the only thing that the authors should consider changing when submitting the manuscript to another journal. Authors need to review the new journal that is being considered as a potential publication outlet and make changes based on its own policies regarding length and style. If the work is interdisciplinary and addresses multiple concepts and theoretical perspectives, the literature review and discussion may need to be revisited to emphasize some elements more than others for the new journal's audience. For example, we frequently have written on nonprofit organizations and public relations concepts together. When submitting a manuscript to a public relations journal, those topics are going to serve as primary literature review topics and take more space while the nonprofit elements will take a secondary role. If that manuscript were rejected by a public relations journal and revised for a nonprofit communication journal, significant time would be focused on reframing the manuscript, featuring the nonprofit elements, while the public relations perspectives take a backseat in the text. Authors should always consider the readership of journals when they're preparing their manuscript, especially when sending it to a second- or third-choice journal after a rejected review.

As you revise, remember that editors look for other articles that have been published in that journal, which shows that the authors have reviewed the journal for the appropriateness of fit for their submitted manuscript and boosts the citation metrics for that journal (related to journal rankings). While there is no magic number of citations, authors should work to include the relevant articles and authors from that journal in their manuscript.

Stage 7: Work Required after the Manuscript Is Accepted

The work is not done when your manuscript accepted for publication. Inevitably, you will need to fix minor errors that were overlooked in the submission process. Often, the editorial staff at the publication house will be able to address issues of spelling and grammar, but you will typically receive article proofs, with inserted tables and figures, and formatted to the specifications of the journal. You will review these proofs, fix any errors, and answer questions that the editor may have. Typically, you have a short turnaround so that the article can be published online promptly and put in the queue ready to be published in the physical journal.

Once the proofs have been accepted by the editor, the article will frequently appear online as an "Online First" publication. This is a digital version of the article that makes it available for the public to read before it is physically printed. (We have waited as long as two years before an accepted manuscript was actually available in the printed journal!). People who subscribe to that journal or who have access to the journal through an association membership or their institutional library databases will be able to read the journal article online immediately once the editor accepts the corrected proofs, so another big task after receiving the acceptance of the manuscript is to make sure you share the article.

Share the news that your manuscript is available online so people will read it, through your college's e-mail announcement listserv, academic social media accounts like Academia.edu and other outlets. You may also want to consider linking your institutional e-mail address to a *Google Scholar* account so that it can track your complete citation history of that particular article as well as all of your publications.

Stage 8: Updating Your CV to Reflect Various Stages of Research Projects

Professionally speaking, there may be no bigger sense of relief than when a manuscript is submitted to a conference or journal. The hours that have been poured into developing the manuscript and editing the content so that it fits the guidelines are plentiful, and the proverbial light at the end of the tunnel is often—and should be—celebrated with special rewards to continue the personal motivation to keep going. With a well-rounded research agenda, the projects never end. Continue to have several other projects in various stages to pick up and continue work on those once another project moves into the review process. Make sure to keep track of your projects and their stages to make sure your research pipeline doesn't run dry. Academics often update their departmental website with projects they're working on as well as their curriculum vitae (CV). The complete citation of your work should be provided with article title, journal name, volume, issue and page numbers for publications, and division and association name, city of conference and dates of the conference for presentations. For works that have been accepted but haven't yet been published or presented, list that work as accepted for publication/presentation, along with a link to the advanced online publication or conference listing, if one is made available. Be careful about listing works in progress. Be honest with the manuscript status and don't include the journal's name until the manuscript is accepted.

CONCLUSION

While service and teaching assignments may change regularly as a professor, the research requirements and expectations will always be there. Hopefully this chapter has helped in providing some information that will better prepare you for becoming a well-rounded researcher. The hardest part of becoming a researcher is figuring out what interests you the most so that you want to investigate it further. Once that hurdle is cleared, research ideas will start coming to your mind in many different situations. You may even start seeing research projects in your everyday, non-research life as you start to envision how variables might be measured in a particular situation in current news events or even in how hobbies and extracurricular events intersect with your research world. While the plethora of ideas may help you broaden and expand your research agenda, it is important to remember to balance research with everything else and sometimes say no to projects at times.

As outlined in this chapter, developing collaborative networks and seeking research funding will strengthen your role as a researcher and scholar. They will also help keep your research pipeline full so that you will be ever present at conferences speaking on panels and giving presentations and throughout the various stages of the publication process. Whether you decide to pursue journal articles, book chapters or entire books, you will develop a strong voice that represents you on different theoretical perspectives. Graduate school and the classes provide a great foundation for beginning that exploration and developing your voice. If you have yet to take on a major research project, find the topic that you're curious about and sketch out a research project. Don't take on too much so that it becomes unmanageable. Remember, no piece of research resolves everything. Research that is done well should help answer questions, fill in some of the gaps in the literature and ultimately raise other questions. Sharing those insights through publications and presentations helps inform others about the topic and helps create your reputation as a scholar and focus your research agenda.

While it may seem difficult to imagine what your future research agenda will look like as a graduate student, going through the research process with your professors, mentors and peers will provide incredible learning opportunities in or out of the classroom. Figuring out how to create multiple papers from research projects and taking those papers through the publishing process with them will grow your confidence. Remember, you only have your first publication once.

8

Navigating the Job Market
Basic Mechanics and Peculiarities
David D. Perlmutter, Texas Tech University

The academic job market has similarities to other kinds of employment-seeking adventures, but it has its own peculiarities as well. As a graduate student, you will probably get a chance to pick up on some of the latter, but others may continue to remain mysterious or about which you may even get conflicting advice. I approach this chapter with the perspective of someone who got his PhD more than 25 years ago from the time of this writing (2020), obtained a tenure-track position while finishing his dissertation, got tenure early, received full professor promotion early, and has served in various administrative positions across four different universities.

I also have written for almost 20 years for *The Chronicle of Higher Education*, focusing on academic careers. The theme of my elected presidency of the Association for Education in Journalism and Mass Communication (2019–2020) has been helping our members advance their careers. Finally, I have written a book about promotion and tenure.[1]

I *do not* offer these credentials to designate myself an all-knowing sage; there are none. But I have had the opportunity over the years to talk to thousands of professors and graduate students at my own universities and many others, prepping for my columns or in reaction to them, so I appreciate how intimidating and quixotic the academic job market can be. The following advice should be considered then with a grain of salt and a degree of cynicism. The tactics enumerated below will at best improve your chances on the academic job market, but there are no guarantees and many variables affect the outcome.

THE BASIC MECHANICS OF THE ACADEMIC JOB SEARCH

The rest of this chapter will focus on some of the special topics of job searching in academia in depth. But since, if you are reading this, it is probably your first ride in the rodeo, I want to go into step-by-step detail of the basic checklist of what you need to do from Day One on the job market.

Let's begin with the basic timeline/stages of looking for an academic position, which may play out over a whole year as opposed to the "two-week" window typical of the private sector.

- During your doctoral studies, you start to develop an interest in pursuing the path to professor or going to work in the government (nonacademic), private or nonprofit sector.
- A further refinement is if you want to work as an academic, what kind of institution would you aim toward? One that perhaps focuses more on teaching, or a more heavily research-oriented university?
- As discussed below, you try to develop contacts, a network of people who might help you, with recommendations and even insider lobbying once you are on the job market.
- Even early and in the middle of your doctoral program, you join professional academic organizations and start perusing the job ads, thinking ahead about which ones might eventually interest you.
- In the year before you graduate, you start actively pursuing job prospects. Under the mentoring of your advisors or other good sources, you specifically identify positions you want to pursue. During that year as well, you try to attend conferences where there are "job hubs" and at which you participate in early interviews. Remember that, in academia, we do everything far ahead. Thus, an interview for, say, a position that starts at the beginning of an academic year in August or September might actually take place in October of the previous year.

Now, some individual tips for key parts of the process. Above all, *get organized*. Create a spreadsheet in Microsoft Word or Excel, wherever you are most comfortable. The columns might include the titles of job positions you plan to apply for, their location (department, university, city), the relevant contact information for the search chair and where you are supposed to send your materials (typically a letter of application, a CV, a teaching statement, letters of references, names and separate contact information for references). Also, you should include columns for the timetables of the search. When are the application materials due? By what date will decisions be made? When will phone and then separate on-campus interviews be conducted?

Next, step back and *determine who you are in the job classifications*. For instance, you will likely never see an ad for "Renaissance Woman." All fields have become specialized in research but—and this is a major nuance—often programs are seeking someone who can teach in more than one area. Also, departments with limited hiring abilities may try to cram two positions into one. So look at job ads and determine which labels fit your background and CV. Know that what a committee thinks is plausible will circumscribe your horizons. If your dissertation and all your conference presentations are on international communication and diplomatic crises, a committee might not buy that you can be a candidate for their "sports media" position.

Now, you should decide *where you are going to look for job announcements*. Job ads in academic fields can be found in four main locations.

First is the proverbial grapevine. Somebody that you have connected with in your networking, at conferences or online, lets you know that a position is open or will be open in their department. Or maybe you simply saw it in a jobs wiki site or in some other social media arena.

The second location is more traditional. Every field has professional organizations that hold conferences and have paper or online (or both) newsletters that contain job ads. In the field of communications, there are quite a number of smaller special-interest organizations, but the big four are National Communication Association, International Communication Association, Broadcast Education Association, and Association for Education in Journalism and Mass Communication. The last is probably the best known for its very active onsite "job hub"—more on that later in this chapter.[2]

A third location for ads is the selection of the big academic news magazines and online resources, such as *The Chronicle of Higher Education* and *Inside Higher Education*. These tend to have fewer ads at the assistant professor level since they are expensive to run, but a university might take out one big ad for all of its open positions.

A final location for job ads may be determined by your demographics. Many universities are often required to take out job ads in publications aimed at minorities, like, say *Insight into Diversity*.

Now you are ready to begin your search. However, other challenges and nuances remain.

CONTEXT: THE VAGARIES OF ACADEMIC HIRING

One of the cruelest realities of academic hiring is that you may never be told what you did objectively "wrong" to lose the job (e.g., your research presentation was incoherent, your teaching background did not include the preferred key courses). Then again, you may have done nothing wrong but failed to get the job for spurious reasons (for example, the winning candidate was the advisee of the search chair's old pal). The interpretation of HR rules, the fear of legal liability and a general reluctance to "make people feel bad" leads to radio silence for failed candidates. At the end of the day (and to borrow from the book of *Ecclesiastes*), you should accept that "the race is not to the swift, nor the battle to the strong ... but time and chance happeneth to them all." You can do everything "right"—presupposing that you even know what "right" is in a particular situation—and still not get the job for unfair, random or illogical reasons. (Or, someone else was better than you *in the qualities sought*, or there was a perceived better "fit" with the position, the unit and the campus.)

You just don't know.

Next, search processes are designed and run by humans and are thus subject to many uncertainties and quirks. Search committees make mistakes, and few searches are clockwork-efficient. Usually, malice is not the cause of your woe, angst or frustration, but rather people are busy and distracted or simply have little experience in the best practices for a search. So, if a search seems awry, it may have nothing to do with you (even though it affects you).

Finally, while much of what is discussed below is particularly relevant to the academic job market, many points can apply to securing careers in the private sector or noneducational nonprofits, or even university positions that are nonacademic. For example, the advice about networking can apply to a graduate student pursuing a job in industry as much as for a job on the tenure track. Accordingly, I will close this chapter with some specific suggestions about seeking nonacademic positions.

But before we dive into searching itself, let's review some preliminary steps grad students often don't think about; these are things you can do in grad school that will help your future searching.

KEEP YOUR EYE ON THE PRIZE IN GRAD SCHOOL

Graduate school can be a confusing place, and it can be easy to get lost and even forget about why you are there and what your priorities are. It is perfectly fine, even commendable, to be motivated to gain knowledge, skills and insights to study something you love, but the impractical graduate student may end up with nothing much to show from her or his time spent pursuing a passion. You must always have a utilitarian streak and remind yourself that all of this hard work you have completed, the energy spent and the stress endured has a tangible final goal.

From a very sensible standpoint, that outcome is *middle-class employment*. For many doctoral students, the means to that end is status as a full-time faculty member—or even better, tenure-track status—at a university, although there may be stops along the way (for example, a stint as a postdoc). But it is absolutely imperative that, when undertaking (or being asked to undertake) any particular activity in graduate school, you can positively answer the question: "Is this action helping me achieve my goal?" Let's suppose you have a social-scientific focus in a field such as communications or sociology or political science, and you want to get a tenure-track job at a top research university. You will have to finish a dissertation (more on that later). That dissertation will need to consist of units that are publishable, preferably in top journals. This means that in graduate school, whenever you are taking a class, you should be thinking about what you learn in the class, either in concept or in writing, as something that eventually will be published.

Note that while "help to achieve my goals" is a call for ruthless pragmatism, many actions that may propel you might not seem that pragmatic on the surface. Exercising, meditating, volunteering at a cat shelter—these activities may not be listable in your CV, but they can help you gain the steadiness of mind to focus on your career purpose. On the other hand, regularly going out to drink to senselessness with a group of other grad students who do nothing but complain about unsolvable issues won't help your future career or your mental or physical health. You must decide, but always remind yourself why you are in grad school.

In short, the "job hunt" begins on your first day in grad school.

PRACTICE SMART NETWORKING WHENEVER YOU CAN

The word "networking" is a controversial one when applied to academics. We rightfully think that we should get something as important as a job based upon our qualifications alone, including how well we do in the interviews and presentations. However, the fact remains that all employment in all careers has a "who-you-know" factor. Academia is absolutely subject to this bias; all the more reason to understand that your job hunt actually begins long before you formally send out applications.

Just to take an example: Imagine sitting in a search committee. Depending on the field/position/location/institution, you might get between 40 and 400 applicants. As those of us who have experienced searches often say, if we were just looking at CVs, we could hire 20 to 30 percent of the people who apply. The quality of the letter (or the teaching statement or even the interviews and the presentation) will certainly narrow the field, but familiarity still matters. It's helpful when you notice a name you recognize and remember that this is a graduate student who had contacted you, with whom you spent an enjoyable 20 minutes at a conference answering questions about your research, but who also impressed you with their line of inquiry. Or, this is the graduate student who, early on, showed up to all of the meetings of a specialty division of your academic professional association and volunteered for additional duties, performing them at a high level. Or perhaps, the letter of recommendation is from somebody you know in the field whose judgment you trust as being a robust spotter and trainer of talent.

All of these little advantages for academic (as well as nonacademic) hiring can add up. The more networking you do—judiciously—the more you will increase your chances of establishing the personal connection that gives you a small inside edge when you are on the job market.

USE THE DISSERTATION AS A TOOL TO GET THE RIGHT JOB

The following is an unfortunately all-too-common tale. A doctoral student is struggling to finish his dissertation. He's on deadline. He is faced with a massive amount of work. He has become extremely stressed and even bored with his own work; all he yearns to do is finish and get on with it. So he produces a "dead-ender." These sad documents almost always share the following characteristics:

- They are short. Some dissertations, shorn of tables, citations, charts and illustrations, probably would not equal the prose volume of an issue of *Teen People* magazine.
- They are one-note analyses. Each is basically a study—usually an experiment or a survey—of one population, asking essentially one set of questions, with outcomes easily summed up in a few sentences.
- They offer only a minor variation on a narrow field of study. Judging from their references, citations and quotes, it is clear that they are purely derivative of existing theory and research.
- They are poorly written. That's probably not because the authors are bad prose stylists but because they are rushed. Their wording often seems insufficiently fleshed out.

These students do *finish*. So one step is achieved ... but not that end goal! A committee—perhaps jaded, distracted, resigned, sympathetic or all of the above—passes the candidate. But a few years later, the new "Dr." realizes his dissertation didn't produce the anticipated number of publishable papers or did not become a book or did not really serve in a practical manner the way it should for success within a given discipline.

So, no matter how mired you are in the mud of completion, always think about the outcomes. Will your dissertation (a) be something that will pass and get you your degree, (b) help you get a desirable job and (c) help you afterward on the tenure track?

LEARN TO DECIPHER JOB AD JARGON

Everyone knows that each academic field has created its own nomenclature, patois and dialect of terminology. But when you start to read academic job ads, you will find that there are many words and phrases that may have cryptic meanings, mean more than one thing or mean something very specific in a local context. Deciphering what exactly is being said is a first step to a successful application for the position. Over the years, I have studied the language of job ads and found that the codes used were almost like trying to resurrect a dead language with a cracked Rosetta Stone. But below are some of the more common words and terms you will come across along with brief definitions. (For more details, see the articles cited.)

"Required" qualifications are those you must demonstrably possess to even be considered as a candidate, let alone to be hired for the job (and approved by HR). Sometimes the requirement applies to the here and now: "at least five years' teaching experience in the field of X." At other times, it is anticipatory: "must have doctoral degree officially awarded by 2021."

"Preferred," on the surface, means, "It would also be nice if you had this." Most job candidates assume, correctly, that the more of these preferred qualifications you have, the better, but not having all of them will probably not be fatal to your candidacy. On the other hand, if you added value with some of the other traits and skills requested, it might get you the job over someone else.

Another term that pops up is "demonstrated commitment" to something. But what that commitment means and how you can show it (or indicate you might develop it) varies. Take the phrase, "demonstrated commitment to teaching." Few academic programs delight in hiring people who implode in the classroom. You often need to show that you care about teaching, and not just rhetorically. State your teaching credentials, but don't just list the courses you've taught or TA'd for. Cite any efforts you made to improve the quality of your teaching, such as workshops you attended. Share any high evaluation scores you received.

Pull out strong examples of your teaching having a positive effect. Share a story about a particular student you engaged.

On the other hand, an ad that mentions a "demonstrated commitment to research" is trickier. If you are applying for a postdoc or tenure-track position at a major research university, asserting your love of scholarship is clearly insufficient. Quality counts, of course. One signal publication in a top journal may outshine a brace of them in lower-ranked journals. Your track record also should be "ascending"—that is, your publications should be growing in number or in prestige from year to year. Finally, make clear that your research is part of a consistent strategy, not just scattershot and opportunistic. What is your five-year productivity plan?

A newer category is "demonstrated commitment to diversity and inclusion." You may be asked to comment on how you have assisted and addressed diversity issues. Many people, especially early in their careers, will draw a blank in this category. They haven't served on a diversity committee or task force or helped to craft a diversity policy. But you may have served on other committees—for example, as the graduate student representative on a search committee—where these issues arise. Perhaps you were a teaching assistant in a diverse classroom. Reference those experiences. If your research touches on diversity issues, mention that.

TAILOR YOUR MATERIALS TO THE PLACE AND POSITION

Obviously, it would be fantastic (although seemingly just a fantasy) that when you are on the job market, you end up receiving multiple offers. It is not so crazy an expectation. If you are good enough for one school to hire you, then you are good enough for others, chance and circumstance permitting. That said, every program to which you apply for a position likes to feel special. I use the analogy of a marriage proposal, and it is not as strained as it may sound. Would you want someone to propose to you generically, as in, "I just want to get married. You'll do, but so will anyone else who says yes"? You probably want something a little more personal and targeted: What makes *you* the *one*?

Likewise, the search committee, the chief administrator and the faculty of the place at which you want to work need to perceive and be demonstrably shown that you want to work for *them*. Yes, they understand that you are on the job market and are probably applying elsewhere. But (see the section on "fit" below) they would like you to prove that you have done research on how good a match you are for the position, the program and even the people and the place. You can draw some key words and phrases from the job ad, but you should also be scouring their website and, if you have any personal connections with faculty or students, getting intel from other sources.

Among the points you could make in this category would be, for example, the specific classes you see yourself being able to teach for them. So don't just say, "I have had experience professionally and in teaching Intro to PR classes." Instead, get into detail and state, "Examining the syllabi of your PR 1131, 1132, and 1133 undergraduate sequence, I am confident that I could teach any of those classes or all of them…" Or, in the category of research, say, "I am familiar with your health communication research team, and the work being done by Professors Prishnamurthy, Goldman and O'Houlihan. I am also very attracted to your health comm. lab." And so on.

So keep it professional—it is obviously *not* an actual marriage proposal—but do personalize your application.

Also, if you want the search committee to know that something is really important to your candidacy, make sure that it is absolutely clear and repeated. The required qualifications are good examples. You will want to note in your letter, for instance, that "my dissertation will be completed on June 20." On your CV, underneath the listing of your dissertation, you should repeat, "planned completion date June 20." And your references, with your prompting, could mention, "I am confident he/she will complete the dissertation by June 20." Yes, overkill, but often overkill is indispensable.

The application letter itself is a stress-inducing exercise. It would be wonderful if you could just write a generic letter about yourself and send it to all the places to which you will apply. (There are sites, like Interfolio, where you can, in fact, do this, but as said, people want to feel special, and they want to feel that you are proposing to them and not to just anyone.) So create a master or template letter, but then tailor it to the individual position, place and people. Why do you want to teach and research technical communication at Illinois State? What is it about Cal Polytechnic's comm program that attracts you? What major research initiatives are going on at Texas Tech that you feel you can help with and be a part of? What specific strengths do you have that fit the open position in public relations at Roger Williams University?

Another major component of your application is your CV. Please recognize that, especially if you are beginning your career, we realize that it will not be voluminous and will contain many empty slots. However, the CV is significant particularly in that it will back up what you and your references say about you, helping answer the "who you are" question.

Another plain fact is that there is an arms race now even at the earliest stages of an academic career. When I was on the job market in 1995, I had two publications as a doctoral student. This was considered admirable. Now, at the Carnegie Tier One University where I am serving as dean, we are hiring fresh-out-of-graduate-school faculty for assistant professor positions who have dozens of conference papers, boast four to five publications, and have at least participated in applying for or working on major grants. As I joke, I'm not sure my 1995 self could get a job at the college where I am a dean in 2020.

Then there are the references. Sometimes, the search committee will ask for (two to three) letters of reference upfront. At other times, they will simply request contact information for someone to speak as a reference via a phone call. Sometimes, both processes will occur. The same perspectives and context about search committees apply to your references. They may be very friendly and supportive, but they are also probably busy, distracted professors with other things going on in their professional lives. Additionally—and people don't like to talk about this—writing a letter of reference, and especially writing lots of letters of references, can be time-consuming and tedious. We are happy to do it for you but may not be very happy about the process itself. So you want to help your reference writers as much as possible to do the job well and efficiently.

First, ask people to write a letter of reference or act as a reference only if they are ready and able. "Ready" means that they give you the impression that they really will do it and they want to do it and you are not dragging them to do it. They actually support you and have strong good intentions about you. You do not want a mediocre letter, especially nowadays when it is generally assumed that many letters are over-the-top and excessively fulsome in praise. So, if we get a letter that is anything less than highly praising, it makes it look really bad for you.

Alternately, a possible reference may be ready and willing but unable—that is, lacking the time for the level of focus. Yes, you will find many well-meaning but absent-minded professors out there. However, you can probably pick up on the reputation of people from other doctoral students. Do they follow through on what they promise?

How can you help goose these potential references to quality completion? Make sure they have all of the information in front of them needed to write the letter or be a good phone reference. A checklist of things to send them might include the job position ad, some notation about what skill sets or achievements of yours fit the position that they can remark on, a reminder of any projects or successes you had with them in your research, and/or any testimonials of superlative teaching or service that they can mention. The key point here is that the letter or the oral recommendation should be tailored to some extent but probably cannot be as much as will your own communications. In the case of a very busy faculty member, you may have to accept a template letter, but you can try to help with as many details as possible.

BE AS FLEXIBLE AS YOU CAN ABOUT WHERE TO APPLY

You no doubt have a master list in your head of "the places you'll go," to quote that Dr. Seuss book your aunt gave you when you graduated from high school. You would like a certain type of position upon graduation from your doctoral program. For example, you may aspire to go directly to the tenure track at a prestigious research university. Even more likely, you may also have a locale or an environment that attracts you. My friends in certain parts of the country known for their natural beauty or skylines or nightlife tell me that they get two to three times more applicants for open positions than do other institutions simply because they are in an aspirational location. More people want to live in Boulder (or "Boulder-adjacent," considering the cost of living in Boulder) than in Muncie or Lubbock.

Then there is family. My sense is that the current generation of doctoral students in their late 20s and early 30s is much more attuned to securing the support and connections for their family than my generation of faculty ever was. Perhaps this is in anticipation or in realization of raising children, or perhaps it's because of the increasing challenge of supporting aging parents or having some other health, family or personal issue that makes staying connected to one's roots peculiarly attractive.

In short, you may have very good reasons to limit your job search to certain kinds of institutions and certain kinds of places. I can't speak much to the former condition since your preference about the kind of place at which you picture yourself on the faculty is something that deeply impacts your professional life, but I can speak to the second kind of limitation, that of the geographic location of your next position. Think about why you're limiting your search. Make a realistic assessment of the jobs and the types of institutions you're interested in.

In a past essay, I wrote about the case of North Dakota, which is probably pretty low on a list of aspirational locations unless you have family in the area. Why wouldn't you want to live someplace like that? Are you imposing class, regional or political prejudices without investigation? Have you ever actually visited Fargo or only seen the movie (which was not set there, anyway)? Have you talked with someone there, like an assistant professor, for eyewitness testimony?

Whatever your discipline or preferred research method, you probably believe it is a good idea to look into something before pronouncing expertise on it. Similarly, once you know more about a given location, you can appraise aspects that might grow on you. When I worked at the University of Iowa (situated in Iowa City), we had a saying: "If we can just get them to visit, they will want to stay." Some job finalists from the coasts stereotyped Iowa as a backwater, but after they visited and found a decent economy, affordable housing, low crime rates, a booming "creative corridor," plenty of arts, music and entertainment, a low-stress off-work life, a very civil society—they ended up remaining for a lifetime.

So, consider: Must you like *every* feature of a place to want to work there?

PRACTICE YOUR JOB TALKS AND PRESENTATIONS FOR A CRITICAL AUDIENCE

One of the most enlightening preparatory experiences you can undertake to get set for your sojourn on the job market is to witness other people's presentations or even to read over their applications. It is very likely, for example, that in the department where you are studying, PhD students will be invited to hear candidates' job talks, typically presentations on teaching or research. Attend, if possible. What you will quickly pick up on is how many mistakes are easy to make when you are a rookie. You will see the underconfident, nervous candidate who hides behind the monitor and mumbles. You will raise an eyebrow at the wildly overconfident candidate who alienates most of the people in the room by overstating claims about his or her skill sets and talents. You will observe how people can get bogged down in details or be too vague in general; perhaps they are too cringy and slavish, or, on the other hand, too defensive or nonresponsive. Mistakes will abound, and you will learn from them about what to do and what not to do. Watching other people is a form of instruction for yourself.

At the same time, nothing beats personal rehearsal and practice for your own presentations. Here is where I have noticed a problem over the years. Doctoral students (or really anyone on the job market) will practice for a few friends ... and there's the rub. Are your friends going to be a truly critical audience? (The word "critical" is meant in the ancient sense, to describe someone who is willing and qualified to help you improve your activity.) So, for example, is your set of four 27-year-old friends an authentically helpful group to give you a sense of what the silverback full professors in the hiring department will be thinking and expecting of you? Are your friends willing to tell you that you are making some mistakes and coming off badly? This is why, if at all possible, it would be optimal for you to recruit some faculty and graduate students who fit the demographic profile of a hiring faculty and committee and who are also willing to give you "tough love" advice.

DOS AND DON'TS FOR THE CAMPUS INTERVIEW

Some other "dos" and "don'ts" that I have experienced and witnessed over some 27 years of being a candidate myself and assessing others:

- Dress appropriately for interviews and presentations. It is always good to err on the side of being a bit too formal than to throw people off by being too casual.
- Remember that you are always on stage. I have seen candidates make grave errors at lunch or being driven around campus because they thought that what they said was not part of the interview or "wouldn't matter." Especially in small towns, where a lot of colleges are located, everybody knows everyone, so always be "on."
- Administrators do not like surprises. If there is something that you will need to be successful on the job—including a spousal issue, for example—it is better to be upfront than to spring something on them later.
- Just like you tailored your application materials, when you show up to campus for a finalist interview, know as much as you can about their program, their mission and their aspirations. You do not have to be overly personal or intrusive, but showing that you read up on the faculty can't hurt.
- Try to get a sense of the culture, not just the facilities and the program. Sometimes, not getting a job offer is like dodging a bullet if it's a toxic atmosphere. If people seem stiff and guarded or don't seem to be communicative to each other, take that as red flags waving.

APPRECIATE THE SIGNIFICANCE OF "FIT" AS WELL AS CREDENTIALS

Reminding ourselves that search committees and administrators are people, it's always important to understand that they are looking for the right sort of person *for them*. For example, some programs really like the idea of hiring a doctoral student fresh from school, so this type of candidate may be more attractive than someone who is better published but who has been on the job market for five years. The latter may be perceived as being past the "freshness date." Unfair, possibly; also not uncommon.

So when you apply to any program, how can you investigate the local fit and culture? Good intel is useful, so try to find out (maybe indirectly) from people who know somebody there or, better yet, from someone at that program you know personally who is willing to tell you about the local culture and what they're looking for in the person and not just the CV.

Please note: You shouldn't try to twist yourself into a pretzel or feign being something that you're not. It is often said that you should be yourself at job interviews, but your *best* self. I would add you should emphasize qualities in your personality that best fit the local culture.

At some point, if you think it's too much of a stretch to be the kind of colleague that they're looking for, you might reconsider pursuing that position.

THINK BEYOND THE ACADEMIC JOB MARKET

If you read *The Chronicle of Higher Education*, the job blogs and wikis, and other academic hiring social media (a practice I strongly encourage), you are no doubt aware that many fields are going through a crisis of employment. Basically, we are producing many more PhDs than can be accommodated by the number of traditional tenure-track positions. In some fields such as history or languages, the situation has gone past crisis to catastrophe. In other fields (such as communications), we have enjoyed, as of this writing in early 2020, a relative boom. So getting a PhD in communications means that you probably can expect a pretty good set of opportunities to teach full-time. The catch is likely that you won't have exactly the job you want at exactly the institution and location you most desire.

Some areas of the academy have traditionally been open to, and done a better job of, preparing students for nonacademic careers. I would say that about one-third to one-half of PhD students in any particular communications cohort decide they aspire to an industry job, typically doing research or policy analysis, or analytics for a corporation, a government agency or a nonprofit. Another big difference in our field is that most of our faculty accept and encourage such an outcome if that is what the student wants.

If you decide that you want a nonacademic position, there are many alt-ac websites and resources to consult. However, generally the same rules and suggestions for making graduate school work for your academic appointment apply to nonacademic appointments. Take networking, for example. My father worked for most of his career as a professor at a leading business school. Hundreds of students did MBAs or undergraduate theses under his guidance and his advice was very utilitarian: Write your project or your report on the industry and the job that you want. As part of your research, connect with the people you want to network with: Interview them, consult them, get to know them, attend their meetings. Then, when you are on the job market, they will know your name and you will have materials to show them of relevance to positions open.

Likewise, if you know that you are going into industry, make sure that, while writing your dissertation, you think in terms of corporate-sector publishable units. How can you help a company, a government department or a nonprofit? Perhaps publish in trade magazines or pull out executive reports that get attention, maybe even modern social media postings from a blog, or a YouTube how-to. Establish that you can produce nonacademic information and analysis.

These are times of uncertainty in higher education, and graduate students are well aware of the big problems, such as those of budgets and enrollment, that many programs are facing. Moreover, this is an unprecedentedly precarious time for navigating the job market. At the end of the day, remember that, although you will have supporters, friends, loved ones, mentors and collaborators who will help you, you steer the helm of your own ship.

FURTHER READING

This essay was drawn from almost 20 years of writing for the *Chronicle of Higher Education*. Among the essays that most inspired the present writing were the following:

David D. Perlmutter. "Career Lingo, pt. 7: 'You Did Great!'" *Chronicle of Higher Education VITAE*, July 20, 2016. https://chroniclevitae.com/news/1489-career-lingo-you-did-great.

David D. Perlmutter. "Your Unofficial Job-Application Checklist." *Chronicle of Higher Education*, November 23, 2012, pp. A27–28.

David D. Perlmutter. "Your Official Job-Application Checklist." *Chronicle of Higher Education*, October 26, 2012, pp. A35–36.

David D. Perlmutter. "Embrace Your Inner North Dakotan." *Chronicle of Higher Education*, August 17, 2012, A21–22.

David D. Perlmutter. "Avoiding Bad Advice from Your Colleagues." *Chronicle of Higher Education*, March 4, 2013 [online].

David D. Perlmutter. "In Search of a Good Critique." *Chronicle of Higher Education*, February 8, 2013, A23–24.

David D. Perlmutter. "Career Lingo, pt. 11: 'Participate in Multidisciplinary …'" *Chronicle of Higher Education VITAE*, April 11, 2017.

David D. Perlmutter. "Career Lingo, pt. 10: 'Demonstrated Commitment to …'" *Chronicle of Higher Education VITAE*, February 28, 2017.

David D. Perlmutter. "Career Lingo, pt. 9: 'Potential.'" *Chronicle of Higher Education VITAE*, December 21, 2016.

David D. Perlmutter. "Career Lingo, pt. 8: 'Strong.'" *Chronicle of Higher Education VITAE*, August 15, 2016.

David D. Perlmutter. "Career Lingo, pt. 7: 'You Did Great!'" *Chronicle of Higher Education VITAE*, July 20, 2016.

David D. Perlmutter. "Career Lingo, pt. 6: 'Ability to Teach the Following ...'" *Chronicle of Higher Education VITAE*, August 24, 2015.

David D. Perlmutter. "Career Lingo, pt. 5: 'We Will Begin Reviewing Applications ...'" *Chronicle of Higher Education VITAE*, April 13, 2015.

David D. Perlmutter. "Career Lingo, pt. 4: The Search Committee." *Chronicle of Higher Education VITAE*, April 3, 2015.

David D. Perlmutter. "Career Lingo, pt. 3: 'In A Related Field.'" *Chronicle of Higher Education VITAE*, March 16, 2015.

David D. Perlmutter. "Career Lingo, pt. 2.: 'Degree Completed By ...'" *Chronicle of Higher Education VITAE*, February 11, 2015, p. A33.

David D. Perlmutter. "Career Lingo, pt. 1: 'Required' vs. 'Preferred.'" *Chronicle of Higher Education VITAE*, January 23, 2015, p. A33.

David D. Perlmutter. "The Best Problem: Dealing with More Than One Job Offer." *Chronicle of Higher Education*, May 10, 2013, A35.

David D. Perlmutter. "Show Them You Really Want the Job." *Chronicle of Higher Education*, June 22, 2012, A33–34.

NOTES

[1] David Perlmutter, *Promotion and Tenure Confidential* (Cambridge, MA: Harvard University Press, 2010).

[2] Some organizations will not let you look at job ads unless you are a member and some sources of ads in these organizations are likely to yield more hits because of your area of concentration. For example, if you are an organizational communication person getting a PhD in Communication Studies, NCA is more likely to be a good source of open positions than AEJMC. If you are focusing on public relations, then maybe it's the other way around.

9

The Degree and the Job Are Yours. What's Next?

Successfully Transitioning from Student to Professor

Marie Hardin, Penn State University

Each semester, I attend the hooding ceremony for new doctoral graduates across our university. As I look out across the sea of happy, hopeful faces, I appreciate the struggles and sacrifices each graduate has made to reach this milestone. My colleagues and I know from experience, as we've been in their shoes. While I watch these future members of the professoriate walk across the stage, I often wonder: How many of these new PhDs will accomplish their goals and find success on the academic career ladder? And, how many will founder and ultimately fail to meet their potential (and perhaps leave the profession)?

Of course, I hope that all will flourish. The life of a faculty member—no matter how it may feel during Week 14 of a 15-week semester or in the days before a conference deadline—is an enviable one for its freedom and flexibility. And most of us enter this profession with lofty goals: to teach future generations, to do ground-breaking research and to make the world a better place in our own way. But I also know that the choices new faculty members make during the first few years of their careers will, in many ways, determine how much they will thrive.

In this chapter, I'll share practical advice to lay a strong foundation in that first academic job and beyond. If you're preparing for your first job—or you've already unpacked your new office—the tips below are meant to provide some "safety bumpers" as you make decisions about your time and priorities. You're at the beginning of what I hope will be a decades-long journey that is rich and rewarding, so don't expect to fully implement everything I suggest in your first semester! As you acclimate to your new career, prioritize what makes you feel most energized and productive, and expand your list of goals as you move along.

FIND A MENTOR (OR TWO) FOR THIS NEW STAGE

It is likely that during your PhD journey your advisor and other faculty guided and mentored you along the way. Those relationships were critical, helping you make decisions that ultimately led to a job, along with providing you seasoned counsel on such matters as your courses and committee selection, conference attendance and dissertation progress. Those relationships will remain important, as your advisor was once an early-career professor, so can still offer valuable insight and open doors for you. I recall providing my advisor with updates from my new job—and how much pleasure he took in seeing my success. He was eager to continue being of help on such matters as providing nominations for awards and opportunities.

It's time to widen your network of mentors and guides beyond those in your doctoral program. A mentor at your new institution will help you navigate its culture and expectations. Your institution may have a formal mentoring program in place for you when you arrive, as many do. If so, that's a positive for you, as research indicates such programs can help you be more productive as a researcher.[1] If not, ask your department head about the possibility of assigning you a mentor. This person can help you understand how to best meet promotion and tenure demands, steering clear of distracting situations.

Having mentors who know you and/or your institution can be a big factor in how you feel about your work and your job. According to a 2018 survey of thousands of faculty members across the United States, the mentoring of junior faculty is critical. One survey respondent said, "I could not be who I am today, or be the mentor to others that I hope I am, without the influence of the strong mentors that I had."[2] A good institutional mentor can advocate for you, help manage your service activity, and suggest opportunities and resources you might not otherwise know about. Of course, you should also keep your eye out for workshops and seminars also available to new faculty at your place of employment.

You'll also want at least one mentor outside your institution but in your discipline, who appreciates your research agenda and career path. A great way to develop these relationships is through conferences in your field. For me, AEJMC was invaluable for this purpose. At conferences, I met faculty members from across the country who became trustworthy advisors on a number of issues. Sometimes, it was after attending a paper presentation and then following up with an author I admired. The prospect of reaching out (either in person or in an e-mail) to a scholar whose work you find motivating or informative may be daunting, but I encourage you to do it. Most senior scholars are flattered and eager to help! Be sure to have substantive questions based on familiarity with their work. You also need to realize that the onus for staying in touch is on you. But I can tell you, as someone who eventually came to be regarded as a "senior scholar" in my discipline, that I have always enjoyed hearing from other scholars who ask for advice and share their ideas. I rarely turn down an invitation for coffee and a conversation during a scholarly conference, and some of those conversations turned into coauthored papers.

It is also smart to get involved with organizations. Where you can: Be a full participant in the life of the organization, not someone who "parachutes in" to present the occasional scholarly paper. Early in my academic career, I got involved with AEJMC interest groups and divisions attending business meetings and volunteering for service that would connect me with more seasoned members. I knew it would fill the "service" field on my CV and could also help me connect with research partners. I started with the smaller groups where it was easy to get engaged quickly, and I built a reputation as someone who was willing to volunteer. I moved to larger divisions over time, then got involved in work on various committees. I rarely said "no" to an opportunity to serve. (And when I was asked to run for president of the organization, I said "yes" to that, too!). The payoff for me was in friends and contacts across the United States, and great research collaborators.

I sought multiple mentors along the way, depending on my career stage. Early on, it was for help with teaching by sharing syllabi and best practices. Mentors also guided me on the publishing process, guiding me on knowing "when to let go" of a manuscript and the best outlet for submission. After I achieved tenure, others—deans and department heads—provided career advice when I decided to move toward administration. Sometimes, I would ask for mentoring as a swap for departmental, institutional or disciplinary service. For example, when I was asked by my dean, just a few days after earning tenure, to take on the role of "associate department head," I agreed on the condition that he become my mentor. He was surprised at my request, but he agreed to do it. His mentoring was the most valuable I have ever received. He introduced me to his contacts across the field and provided me with challenging and instructive opportunities. That approach—providing opportunity and connections along with advice—has become my "MO" as a mentor. I'd like to think I emulate his mentoring style today with faculty who seek my counsel. When it's your turn to "pay it forward"— and that day will come—you'll be a more effective mentor if you've taken note of the ways others have helped you.

MIND YOUR BUSINESS

More than anything, this might be the most important piece of advice I can provide anyone new to the academy. I often see young scholars trade the business to which they should be paying *very close attention*—how to succeed in teaching, productivity in research and collegiality in service—for things that are most certainly *not* their business. These include interpersonal squabbles among colleagues, administrative issues over which they have no control, curricular matters best left to faculty in a better position to consider them, or activity that, while fulfilling, does not carry help toward tenure (such as volunteering to serve on time-consuming organizational boards when you've been told you have ample service. Do that later!).

I've also seen new professors who erroneously spend a great deal of energy trying to change the priorities of their institution of employment to better match their preferences. That's a waste of time! As a junior professor, attempting to convince your department head or dean that you should be teaching a boutique course that matches your interests but has no fit in the curriculum; should receive course-load releases because of the "special" nature of your research; or should have some other kind of dispensation from institutional norms does nothing to advance your career or help your reputation.

Simply put: The business of a new professor is to learn the priorities and expectations of the institution—and to align their work with it ... or seek a different employer.

So: What does that mean, in practical terms?

- *Read the documents related to tenure and promotion at your institution.* Then, seek guidance from your department head and others who have been promoted on how the documents have traditionally been interpreted. (And, yes: There is more than one way to interpret these documents.)
- *Carve out time to conduct the kind of scholarly activity that will "count" toward tenure.* This oftentimes means making decisions to delay a project you might *like* to do in favor of one that draws on your expertise in a way that your institution values. For instance, you may be in a department where the "coin of the realm" is refereed research in journals. It might be wise to put off the book project you've been mulling in favor of journal-sized projects. That requires discipline and patience. If you're not sure about how to prioritize your research and/or creative activities, seek the advice of senior colleagues and administrators. Then *take the advice* if it makes sense. Perhaps ask

those who have recently been successful in the process if you can see their dossiers.
- *Pay attention and respond constructively to feedback from students about your classes.* At most colleges and universities, teaching excellence is expected and will be central to your duties.[3] Of course, there are other ways to gauge and improve teaching effectiveness, but student ratings are standard for evaluation. As flawed as these mechanisms might be, they are likely integral to the tenure-and-promotion process. If those deciding your fate are paying attention, you should, too—responding to those criticisms and suggestions that appear with any kind of frequency. And, an important point: Student ratings can also be valuable and actually improve teaching! I find that many students want to learn in their classes, and their criticism (or praise) is justified. It's de rigueur among some professors to wear low student evaluations as some kind of "badge of honor," as they imagine that the criticism is because they are demanding of students. But I find that the most demanding professors—if they are *organized* and *fair*—often get the highest ratings from students.
- *Professionally perform the service that is asked of you and seek service that aligns with your expertise.* If you believe service to your institution or to the discipline is getting in the way of your teaching and scholarly activity, seek advice on how to manage priorities. And—although you should use it judiciously—"no" is an option you may sometimes need to use.[4] This is where a good mentor in your department or college can come in handy (see above).

The four key points I just outlined are *your business*. Mind it. Doing well in these areas will take all of your time. The other things, such as getting involved in internecine departmental politics, drain you of the energy you need to succeed.

Early in my career, I was talking about the politics in my workplace to an accomplished colleague, from another university, whom I admired. She listened for a few minutes and then said, "If you don't like what's happening in your department, just close your door and build your empire." That advice immediately resonated with me. She was gently telling me that I—and no one else—was responsible for doing something great with the many opportunities and privileges that come with being a faculty member. I didn't need the permission of anyone to work on becoming a great teacher or to write the kind of articles that would move me toward tenure. No one was forcing me to participate in hallway gossip. Only I could build the record that would both earn tenure and make me attractive to other institutions. Her advice became my silent mantra. I would, after office hours were over, literally close my door and drill down on my goals, which included moving to a university that better aligned with the kind of work I wanted to do.

And that brings me to my next piece of advice.

BUILD A STRONG REPUTATION INSIDE AND OUTSIDE YOUR INSTITUTION

Once you've gotten settled and have a good sense of the culture and priorities for your institution, focus on being a productive, collegial member of the community. Move away from the mindset of a student and transition to a reliable contributor to your unit. You might be surprised at how much is simply "showing up" as a supportive, positive presence. You'll want to ensure that you don't become viewed as a "high maintenance" faculty member among your peers.

For instance, as a person who is relatively low in the "pecking order" among your departmental colleagues, you shouldn't expect to get your pick of class times or room. And while your colleagues want you to feel welcome and comfortable, strongly voiced opinions about curricula or policies at faculty meetings might be viewed with skepticism—considering that you're new. Take the time to wade into the pool. Your colleagues' initial questions about you will be: "Will this person enhance the culture? Can this person deliver on our expectations around teaching, research and service?" Your goal should be to ensure that the answer is yes. At some point—and earlier than you might think—you may decide that you want something different in an academic environment than you initially believed. Your positive relationships where you work will come in very handy. After all, your colleagues will likely someday be references for you, as the likelihood is fairly high that you'll change employers at least once in your career.

I started at a small, private liberal-arts college that focused primarily on teaching. It offered no graduate degrees, and the research requirements were minimal. At the time, I thought this was exactly the kind of institution I wanted, and I thrived. Over a few years, though, I realized that I missed research. Thus, I started positioning myself by building my CV for that move, and I was able to use a few carefully selected peers as references. Soon, I landed at a slightly larger institution with more research support. A few years later, I decided that I wanted to pursue a more comprehensive institution where I could both specialize and have access to a wider array of resources. Again: I "closed my door and built my empire." I had also built a good network of mentors and friends in scholarly organizations—people who knew and respected my work. That helped me land at my current institution, where I've been for more than 15 years.

It took two moves to get here. The lesson: Be patient, meet the expectations of the institution you're at, think about your values and preferences, and work toward getting where you want to be.

HANDLING THE CURVEBALLS

I've provided some practical advice here that, as an administrator, I've seen work for many new faculty. However, I would be remiss if I didn't recognize that the best-laid plans can be thwarted by luck or chance. Your first job, for instance, might be one in which you discover that the department head is ineffective, unavailable or unhelpful. There are also conditions that are out of our control, such as the economy's impact on the job market or on conditions for higher education where you work. Your first job might be one that you know, even before stepping into it, is not a match for you, but it was all that was available. Family considerations might limit or even dictate the geographic area in which you must work. If you find yourself in a situation where you must make the best of a poor working environment (perhaps indefinitely), there are some things you can do for yourself. Those include the following.

Do the work that will get you noticed beyond your immediate environment. It's difficult to look beyond your current demands, but you must, if you are to improve your situation. Draw from the well of self-discipline that got you through your PhD to set goals that will get you noticed among your disciplinary peers. This extra effort can open doors you never anticipated—for fellowships, grants and other perks that might give you leverage in your own unit or provide resources that would make things better for you. But there is no substitute for the high-quality work you need to do *and* the follow-up to have it get noticed (such as asking a mentor to nominate you for an award). It's tempting to spend all of our energy on addressing the present, such as the overflowing inbox or next week's lesson plan.[5] But we must have the discipline to put that aside on a regular basis (Don't worry. It'll still be there!) in pursuit of goals that will ensure a better future.

Expand your network. Even if you realize that you're not in a position to leave, start networking as though you are. Ask your mentors in the discipline to introduce you to people at appealing institutions and don't be afraid to reach out to new contacts via e-mail or social-media platforms (such as LinkedIn) to seek advice or share news so they get to know you. The key is to make time for networking and to approach it with integrity.[6] There are many, many useful articles and guides on networking; read about best practices and adopt those that work best for your style.

Brainstorm solutions to specific barriers you face. If you bring value to your department through consistently reliable productivity as a teacher and scholar, the chances are good that your department head or dean will be eager to find even small ways to make your situation better. I can tell you from experience, however, that they may need your help in obtaining those things, so don't hesitate to ask for resources that could enhance the institutional mission or its visibility. (Note: Parking and office space are generally nonstarters. Your boss likely has far less leverage in those areas than you think!) Also consider what you can do for yourself. Can you rethink your approach to grading that will retain the integrity of your course, but lessen the burden on you? What stress-inducing committees and gatherings could you possible forgo, provided they aren't required for you to be a contributing member of the unit? Identify practical short-term and long-term solutions to the specific obstacles to your goals.

Write it down. It's easy to lose track of the many threads of your job. But chronicling your many accomplishments is critical to the case you build for yourself with your current or future employer. As one author advises:

> Indeed, early-career academics should get in the habit of documenting everything, even if it feels silly to do so. ... Every time you consult on a project or meet with an administrator, make a note of it. When you are nominated for awards, jot it down. You will be glad for the documentation when you prepare your next job-market or tenure-and-promotion files.[7]

Of course, there is more to write down than accomplishments: I have lists of ideas for research, teaching and program ideas. I also keep lists for follow-up projects and with people I've met. There are many ways to do this (and plenty of sources for ideas and advice); find the way that works for you.

Seek and enjoy time away from work. I won't belabor the many adages about what really matters in life; you're familiar with many of them. But I will provide this reminder: If your life outside of work is satisfying, it's far more likely that your worklife will also be gratifying—and vice versa.[8] You have probably heard a lot of chatter in the popular culture about "work–life balance." I prefer to think about the work–life *blend*. The work and "life" of a faculty member do not cleanly divide, especially since so much work sits ready to be addressed via smartphones. Thus, the challenge becomes in creating a holistic life in which you have the time you want and need to enjoy hobbies, family and friends in your community. Even on the tenure track, this is possible—and will make you a more productive and happier faculty member.

CREATING THE LIFE YOU WANT

If you've reached this point in this book, I'm guessing that you are well into your journey in academia and have been able to apply the advice of my colleagues for navigating your path of study, working as a graduate assistant, navigating the conference scene, finishing the degree and landing the first job. Congratulations on the accomplishments that have gotten you here!

If you're like me, you've faced your share of challenges and frustrations along the way. We all have our failures, and we generally do a good job (without any help) of recognizing those. I hope that you've developed the habit of celebrating your successes, even the small ones. They add up: a literature review drafted, a lesson plan completed, a stack of assignments graded, a service project completed, an e-mail box emptied. These may seem like mundane tasks, but they are essential. And they accumulate to help you fulfill your aspirations: to pursue new knowledge, to mentor and teach future generations, to collaborate with colleagues who motivate and inspire you, and to share what you know with your community and with society.

Now is the time: Chart your path and move forward with confidence. Will you have days when you question your career choice? Undoubtedly, yes. But those days will be far outnumbered by those when you will find immense satisfaction in this life you have chosen. Enjoy the journey!

NOTES

[1] Julia Muschallik & Kerstin Pull, "Mentoring in Higher Education: Does It Enhance Mentees' Research Productivity?," *Education Economics* 24, no. 2 (2015): 210–223, https://doi.org/10.1080/09645292.2014.997676.

[2] Karen Webber, *The Working Environment Matters: Faculty Member Job Satisfaction by Institution Type* (March 2018): 18, TIAA Institute.

[3] Marie Iding & R. Murray Thomas, *Becoming a Professor: A Guide to a Career in Higher Education* (Lanham, MD: Rowman & Littlefield, 2015), 109.

[4] Iding & Thomas, *Becoming a Professor*, 116.

[5] Peter Bregman, "You Need to Practice Becoming Your Future Self," *Harvard Business Review*, March 28, 2016, https://getpocket.com/explore/item/you-need-to-practice-being-your-future-self?utm_source=pocket-newtab.

[6] Trenda Boyum-Breen, "Building Your Network," *Inside Higher Ed*, July 19, 2013, https://www.insidehighered.com/advice/2013/07/19/why-networking-matters-and-tips-reaching-out-essay.

[7] Manya Whitaker, "How to Advocate for Yourself as an Early-Career Scholar," *The Chronicle of Higher Education*, July 1, 2018, para. 13.

[8] Belgin Aydintan & Hakan Koc, "The Relationship Between Job Satisfaction and Life Satisfaction: An Empirical Study on Teachers," *International Journal of Business and Social Science* 7, no. 10 (October 2016): 72–80.

Glossary of Academic Terms

GENERAL TERMS

Accreditation a standardized, systematic evaluation of a program or university. Reaccreditation occurs at set intervals, with a clear set of objectives to be met for the program/university to stay accredited.

Carnegie Classification a system for identifying types of institutions, see https://carnegieclassifications.iu.edu/classification_descriptions/basic.php.

Cohort a group of grad students that begin at the same time and move through a program together.

Copy Code a password used for a department's/college's copy machine.

Core Course a required course for a program of study.

Cover Letter a professional letter that accompanies a manuscript, job application or other work. May be digital.

Credit Hours refers to the number of hours that a particular class counts toward the overall degree program requirements.

Curriculum Vitae (CV) the academic résumé. It is much longer than the one-page standard used in industry.

R1 Universities (R1s) institutions with doctoral programs that are known for very high research productivity.

R2 Universities (R2s or Comprehensives) institutions with some doctoral programs that are known for high research productivity.

Small Liberal Arts Colleges (SLAC) smaller, undergraduate institutions that are primarily focused on teaching.

CV Categories

- Education—lists degree, advisor and dissertation and thesis titles.
- Publications—separated into "peer-reviewed" and "other." May have subheads for types of publications (peer-reviewed articles, book chapters, authored books and edited books). Popular works should have their own section.
- Conference Presentations—format like a publication, listing presenters, date, title, group presented to, name of conference, type of presentation and location. If you backed out of a conference (DON'T DO THIS), you may not list the presentation on your CV.
- Teaching Experience—list the names, location and, sometimes, a brief description of the courses for which you were Instructor of Record, a teaching assistant or a lab assistant. Specify your role.
- Grants, Awards and Scholarships—state the name, year, amount (if applicable) and other relevant information.
- Training and Development—any additional enrichment for your academic career. May include courses on pedagogy, workshops, preconference sessions or brown bags.
- Professional Experience—industry (nonacademic) experience that is relevant to your discipline. Don't include, say, your high school cashier job at Subway.
- Service—committee work, as well as manuscript reviewing and other journal and conference roles are stated here. Indicate which level (department, college, university, professional organization).
- Additional Categories—depending on the discipline, you may have sections on relevant skills, language proficiency and other topics.

Discipline a broad field or area, typically connected to an academic department or college.

Elective not a required course but counts toward the program of study. May be outside of the department.

E-mail Query a short, professional e-mail that pitches an article, book manuscript, project, or otherwise serves as an introduction.

Family Educational Rights and Privacy Act (FERPA) a federal law that protects the privacy and confidentiality of grades and other educational documents and records.

Hybrid Course a class that requires a blend of online work with in-person meetings.

Imposter Syndrome feeling like you don't belong or aren't worthy of the position you've been given. This may happen in grad school, as an instructor or on the tenure track. Mentoring can help reassure you that you can do the job.

Lab a hands-on learning format held in a facility different from a typical classroom. Often skills-focused.

Lecture   a larger class in which the majority of instruction comes in the form of lecture presentations.

Mentor   a seasoned person that guides you through a stage of your schooling or career. Can have multiple mentors.

Online Course   a class taken online, with little to no in-person meetings required.

Orientation   a session or sessions held before classes begin that introduces new students to faculty, other students, facilities and key information needed for grad school success.

Prerequisite   a course required before a student can enroll in another course.

Seminar   a smaller class in which the majority of instruction comes in the form of discussions.

Syllabus   a structured overview of the elements in a course, includes instructor information, course objectives, policies, point distribution, assignments, means of assessment and an outline of the topics covered and assigned readings.

Stipend   a set amount of money granted for a specific purpose (i.e., summer research money).

Terminal Degree   the highest degree one can achieve in its particular path: PhD, JD (law degree) and MFA (Master of Fine Arts) are all considered terminal degrees.

Time Management   learning to balance various responsibilities to be successful.

Travel Funding   money granted to reimburse graduate students or faculty for a trip to present papers at academic conferences or for other research/career-related purposes. Travel funding usually involves a series of forms submitted both before the trip and after the trip.

ON PEOPLE AND ROLES

Advisor   the person who formally guides the selection of coursework and later, the thesis or dissertation. Students may change advisors over the stages of a graduate program.

Committee Member/Reader   a peripheral person who gives feedback on a thesis/dissertation but is not the primary advisor. May be from outside the department or area of study.

Tenure   the coveted job category that tenure-track faculty work toward and apply for in their fifth or sixth years. Unlike adjunct, full-time temps and tenure-track assistant professors, tenured faculty are not subject to the same probationary practices, meaning their positions are much more secure. If a tenure-track faculty member does not earn tenure, that person is typically dismissed from the university.

Tenured   a person who has achieved tenure, often with promotion to associate professor rank (and sometimes then promoted to the full professor rank).

Types of Academic Positions

Adjunct a non-tenure-track position, in which a person teaches, but does not typically perform research or service. May be temporary.

Full-Time Temp a non-tenure-track position focused on teaching.

Tenure Track a position in which one is working toward achieving tenure (often in the fifth or sixth year) through establishing excellence in teaching, research and service.

Assistant Professor sometimes called "junior faculty," this is the "starting out" position, working toward tenure through demonstrated excellence in teaching, research and service.

Associate Professor typically a tenured professor, between the ranks of assistant and full.

Full Professor (sometimes just called "Professor") tenured and at the highest rank that a faculty member can achieve.

Graduate Director an administrator that oversees a graduate program. Depending on the structure of the university, this person may report to a department chair/director or to the dean of a college.

HIERARCHY OF ADMINISTRATORS

Department Chair (sometimes called a director) an administrator that oversees an academic department or school.

Dean an administrator that oversees a particular college in a university. The dean is above the department chair in the hierarchy. May have an associate and/or an assistant dean.

Provost an administrator that oversees all the colleges. There may be several vice provosts at a large university (in charge of different areas), but usually one provost.

President an administrator that oversees the whole college or university.

GRADUATE ASSISTANTSHIPS

Graduate Assistant a broad term used to describe graduate students with any kind of assistantship.

Graduate Teaching Assistant (GTA or TA) a graduate student assigned to help a faculty member in a particular undergraduate class. Depending on the program and instructor, duties may include taking attendance, grading, entering grades, making copies, processing scantrons, holding office hours and meeting with students, writing quiz or exam questions, giving guest lectures and/or covering class when the instructor cannot be there.

Graduate Research Assistant (GRA or RA) a graduate student assigned to help a faculty member on a particular research project. Duties may include making copies, recording data, proctoring, running experiments and doing other tasks to support the project.

Instructor of Record the person listed and responsible for teaching a particular class. This may include all of the duties of a regular instructor, including creating a syllabus, assignments and means of assessment, lecturing, meeting with students and assigning grades.

Office Hours a set period of each time each week, in which an instructor (or a teaching assistant) is available to meet with students.

STAGES OF GRADUATE SCHOOL

ABD (also called a "PhD Candidate") All But Dissertation. This term is applied to doctoral students that have passed their coursework and comprehensive exams, leaving only the dissertation to complete.

Coursework the stage of graduate school in which students primarily take classes.

Comprehensive Exams (also called Preliminary or Qualifying Exams) cumulative exams that either measure concepts from a student's coursework/primary areas of study or address mastery of the literature needed for writing the dissertation. May be written, oral or a combination of both.

Thesis/Dissertation Proposal an overview of what a graduate student intends to do for the larger thesis or dissertation. Contains parts of the research paper through the method section. In many programs, students must orally defend their proposals in order for them to advance to conducting the primary research.

Thesis a lengthy research project that contributes new knowledge to an existing body of work. Completed according to a university's set of guidelines and approved by an advisor and selected committee members. This term typically refers to the research project produced at the master's level.

Dissertation an even lengthier research project that contributes new knowledge to an existing body of work. Completed according to a university's set of guidelines and approved by an advisor and selected committee members. Students often take several years to conduct and write up the research for the dissertation. This term typically refers to the research project produced at the doctoral level.

CONFERENCES, PUBLISHING AND THE RESEARCH PROCESS

Abstract a synthesis of a research project, formatted in a paragraph or multiple paragraphs. These range in length, but all should convey the overarching idea, purpose, key findings/results and relevance to the field.

Blind Review a process in which neither the manuscript creator, nor its reviewers, know each other's identities.

Book Chapter a chapter based on research written for a single-authored or edited book.

Call for Proposals (CFP) an announcement of a conference or publication opportunity. Lists the scope and guidelines for the project.

Collaboration/Coauthorship a professional relationship in which two or more grad students or scholars work together on a research project. A coauthored publication has more than one author.

Discussant a person assigned to give feedback for a particular conference paper or set of papers.

Edited Volume an anthology in which multiple scholars contribute chapters around a particular topic. This book is an edited volume.

Exhibit Hall At a conference, usually a big room in which publishers and university representatives set up booths.

Google Scholar One of the premiere web search engines for published academic work. Scholars can create profiles here that track citations and other metrics. https://scholar.google.com/.

Grad-Student Rate discounted prices granted to graduate students for registration.

Interlibrary Loan (ILL) a system connecting libraries all over. Use this resource to get ahold of books and articles outside of your university's collection.

Institutional Review Board (IRB) the university ethics board that oversees all research involving human subjects. This type of research must be *IRB-approved* before data collection begins.

Keynote Speaker the featured speaker that may serve as the opening session at a conference or other event. Usually an important person in the field.

Moderator the timekeeper at a conference session.

Networking informal personal connections that people make with other people.

Parts of a Research Paper (May Vary by Discipline)

Introduction the first section of a paper. Sets up the research study and contains the statement of purpose and justification.

Literature Review the section of the research paper that synthesizes existing literature (published academic articles and books) in such a way that sets up how your project will contribute. Should be well-organized, with topic sentences and subheads to guide readers.

Theoretical Framework the section of the research paper that lays out relevant theories of the discipline, establishing a foundation for the current work.

Method the section of the research paper that outlines the research questions/hypotheses, methodology (what will be done or what was done, drawing from literature in the field), sample and other key information as to how the research will be (or was) conducted.

Sample a part of the Method that specifies what group of information/people/texts/artifacts and so on will be (or was) examined. Explains the parameters for the sample selection.

Findings/Results the section of the research paper that describes what was found/identified/reported from conducting the research. Only include original research here (not secondary literature).

Discussion the section of the research paper that discusses the findings/results. Draws on existing literature (previously published studies) to make sense of what was found and what was not found.

Conclusion the section of the research paper that wraps up the project, looking at its big-picture relevance. Here, the writer may include the limitations and implications for future projects. These two components may also have their own sections.

Peer-Reviewed Journal Article a manuscript that has undergone blind review (often several rounds of it) before being published in an academic journal (or collection of published manuscripts that fit a particular discipline, methodology, issue or subculture).

Popular Articles work that is written for a popular audience and that is published in a nonacademic outlet. Does not undergo the blind peer-review process.

Research Agenda the overarching umbrella of topics that a scholar studies over a long time period. These topics should be connected and related, but do not always cover exactly the same issue.

Revise and Resubmit (R & R) a term used to describe a manuscript status with a journal. R & R means that a manuscript can be revised, per reviewer feedback, and then resubmitted to that journal, at which point, it will be reconsidered for publication.

Scholarly Writing a formal style of writing that appears in academic journals and books. Uses a citation style (i.e., APA, MLA, Chicago, Harvard).

Types of Conference Sessions

Preconference sessions or workshops held before the official start of a conference, clustered around special topics, skills or issues within the discipline. Separate registration and a small fee are often required.

Traditional Research Session Four to five presenters who typically spend 12–15 minutes talking about their own individual papers. These sessions often use PowerPoint and have a moderator and a discussant.

High Density Session (HDS) Eight to ten presenters who typically have 3 or 4 minutes each to give the highlights of their individual research papers in front of a group. No PowerPoint, but may use handouts. Round-table discussions sometimes follow the group presentation.

Scholar to Scholar (also called a poster session) much like a science fair, this format has a room full of scholars standing next to posters they created about their individual papers. Conference goers stroll around the rows of posters and chat with the individual scholars. May have discussants individually assigned to each paper.

Panel Session invited panelists present on a common topic, followed by a moderator-led discussion. Panel proposal deadlines tend to differ from the open research paper competition.

About the Contributors

Denise Bortree (PhD, College of Journalism and Communications, University of Florida) is an associate professor in the Department of Advertising/Public Relations in the Bellisario College of Communications at Penn State University. In addition, she is the director of the Arthur W. Page Center for Integrity in Public Communication. Bortree was the chair of the Professional Freedom and Responsibility (PF&R) committee at AEJMC in 2018–2019. She studies sustainability communication and nonprofit volunteerism.

Jan Lauren Boyles (PhD, Communication, American University; MSJ, West Virginia University) is an assistant professor of journalism/big data at Iowa State University's Greenlee School of Journalism and Communication. Before joining Iowa State, Boyles worked at the Pew Research Center and served as a Google Journalism Fellow. She is the vice chair of AEJMC's Council of Divisions.

Meredith D. Clark (PhD, Mass Communication, University of North Carolina at Chapel Hill; MA, journalism, Florida A&M University) is an assistant professor in the Department of Media Studies at the University of Virginia. She was chair of the Commission on the Status of Women in 2018–2019. Her research focuses on the intersections of race, media and power in journalism and social media spaces.

Katherine A. Foss (PhD, Mass Communication, University of Minnesota) is a professor of media studies in the School of Journalism & Strategic

Media at Middle Tennessee University. She is the head of the AEJMC Council of Divisions. Foss previously edited *Beyond Princess Culture: Gender and Children's Marketing* and *Demystifying the Big House: Exploring Prison Experience and Media Representations*. She is also the author of *Constructing the Outbreak: Epidemics in Media and Collective Memory*, *Breastfeeding and Media: Exploring Conflicting Discourses That Threaten Public Health*, and *Television and Health Responsibility in an Age of Individualism*.

Jennifer Greer (PhD, Journalism and Communications, University of Florida) is a professor and dean of the College of Communication and Information at the University of Kentucky. She served as AEJMC president for 2017–2018, and also headed the Standing Committee on Teaching and the Mass Communication and Society Division. She's been in academic administration for 20 years, including time as graduate director, department chair, interim dean and associate provost at the University of Alabama and the University of Nevada.

Marie Hardin (PhD, Mass Communication, University of Georgia; MA, Communication, Georgia State University) is professor and dean in the Donald P. Bellisario College of Communication at Penn State. She was president of AEJMC in 2018–2019. Her research has focused on journalistic content as it relates to popular sports, and journalistic practice, frequently focusing issues of diversity, ethics and professionalism in sports newsrooms.

Susan Keith (PhD, Journalism and Mass Communication, University of North Carolina at Chapel Hill; MA, journalism studies, University of South Florida-St. Petersburg) is an associate professor and past chair of the Department of Journalism and Media Studies at Rutgers University. She was elected vice president of AEJMC in 2019 and will serve as president in 2021–2022. She studies journalistic content, especially visual content, and journalistic practice, frequently focusing on editing, as well as media ethics and media law.

David D. Perlmutter (PhD, Mass Communication, University of Minnesota) is a professor in and dean of the College of Media & Communication at Texas Tech University. He has been writing about academic careers and campus matters for almost 20 years for *The Chronicle of Higher Education*. In 2010, Harvard University Press published his book on promotion and tenure, and in 2019–2020 he served as president of the Association for Education in Journalism and Mass Communication.

James Stewart (PhD, Communication, University of Southern Mississippi; MA, University of Southern Mississippi) is head of the Department of Mass Communication at Nicholls State University in Thibodaux, LA. He also President of the Association of Schools of Journalism and Mass Communication.

Amanda Sturgill (MS, PhD, Communications, Cornell University). is an associate professor of journalism at Elon University. She is head of the Standing Committee on Teaching for AEJMC and directed graduate programs at Baylor University prior to coming to Elon. She teaches journalism, graduate digital strategy and media analytics. Her scholarship includes work in media and religion, communications pedagogy and news, and new media.

Richard D. Waters (PhD, University of Florida) is the immediate past chair of the AEJMC Standing Committee on Research and member of the Board of Directors. He is currently the chair of the Public Relations Division's Past Heads Committee. His research interests include fundraising, negotiation theory as an approach to understanding major gift donors' charitable contributions to nonprofit organizations, and how organizations develop and maintain relationships with their stakeholders. He is an associate professor at the School of Management at the University of San Francisco.

Index

ABD (all but dissertation), 1, 143
abstracts, 143
academic conferences, 75–92; attire at, 90; cost of, 79; courtesy at, 90; defined, 76–77; divisions, 87; dos and don'ts, 90–91; exhibit halls, 88, 144; financial considerations, 29; grad-student rate, 144; high-density sessions, 82–83, 145; interest groups, 87; job search and, 89; keynote speaker, 144; moderator, 144; new attendees, 86–87; organizational sessions, 86–88; out-of-convention sessions, 89; overview, 11, 75–76, 91; panel sessions, 145; posters, 83–85; preconferences, 145; preparing for, 79–86; presentations at (*See* presentations at academic conferences); protocol at, 90–91; questions at, 90; receptions, 88–89; scholar-to-scholar sessions, 83, 145; selection of, 77–79; socials, 88–89; student participation in, 78, 90–91; taking optimum advantage of, 86–89; traditional research papers, 80–81; traditional research sessions, 145; travel funding, 79–80
accreditation, 139
adjuncts, 142
administrative staff, 19
advisors, 36–41; assignment of, 37; assistant professors as, 39; availability of, 38–39; changing, 40–41; defined, 141; divergence of work and, 38; ideal attributes of, 37; meetings with, 40; professorship, transition to, 130; publishing and, 95–96; requesting, 39–40; respect for work and, 38; tenure and, 39–41; theses and dissertations and, 65, 71
AEJMC. *See* Association for Education in Journalism and Mass Communication (AEJMC)
age differences, 14
Ali, Makkah, 32
American Academy of Advertising (AAA), 77
American Journalism Historians Association (AJHA), 77, 79, 85
American Psychological Association (APA), 76, 106

American University, 63
"Andazuling It!" (podcast), 32
anxiety, coping with: graduate assistants, 57–58; transition to graduate school and, 20–22
application letters, 121
Arthur W. Page Center (Penn State), 101
assistant professors, 142
assistants. *See* graduate assistants
associate professors, 142
Association for Business Communication (ABC), 77
Association for Education in Journalism and Mass Communication (AEJMC): academic conferences, 76–79, 82–91; coursework, selection of, 41; Graduate Student Interest Group (GSIG), 86–87; Job Hub, 89; job search and, 113, 115, 128*n*2; marginalized groups and, 25, 32; Midwinter Conference, 78–79; path of study, selection of, 36; professorship, transition to, 130–31; publishing and, 101; Southeast Colloquium, 41, 76, 78; teaching assistants and, 56; theses and dissertations and, 72; transition to graduate school and, 14, 16
Auburn University, 99
authorship: graduate assistants and, 60; presentations at academic conferences and, 85; in publishing, 67

Bellisario College of Communications (Penn State), 96
Birkenstein, Cathy, 43
Black College Communication Association (BCCA), 77
Black Graduate and Professional Student Association, 31
blind-review, 143
book chapter, 143
Bortree, Denise Sevick, 11, 147
Boyles, Jan Lauren, 10–11, 147

Bradshaw, Amanda, 87
brainstorming solutions, 136
Broadcast Education Association (BEA), 77, 115
Broyles, Sheri, 84
Buddie, Amy M., 76
Bureau of Labor Statistics, 22

calls for proposals (CFP), 143
candidacy, 45
Carnegie classification, 139
Carnegie Classification of Institutions of Higher Education as Research, 101
Chaffee, Steve, 75
Chicago style, 106
Chronicle of Higher Education, 36, 113–14, 126
citation: guidelines of journals, 106; importance of, 54; online cite managers, 43
Clark, Meredith D., 10, 147
co-authorship, 144
cohorts, 139
collaboration: defined, 144; in publishing, 94, 96–97
committee members, 65–66, 141
community connection, marginalized groups and, 31–32
comprehensive exams, 44–45; defined, 143; oral defense, 45; outcomes of, 45; preparing for, 44–45; as stage of graduate school, 6
conclusion section of papers, 103–4, 145
conferences. *See* academic conferences
copy code, 139
core courses, 139
Council of Communication Associations (CCA), 77
coursework: core courses, 139; defined, 143; electives, 41, 140; graduate assistants, balancing coursework, 49; hybrid courses, 140; online cite managers, 43; online courses, 141; other universities, courses at, 41–42; publishing, balancing with, 98–99;

reading in, 42–43; selection of, 41–44; as stage of graduate school, 6; writing in, 42–43
cover letters, 139
Covey, Stephen, 30
credit hours, 139
curriculum vitae: categories of, 140; defined, 139; job search and, 114–15, 117, 121; publishing, updating for, 109–10

data management, 70
deans, 142
departmental organizations, 21
department chairs, 142
DePaul University, 42
different circumstances, 9–10
DiRusso, Carlina, 107
disabilities, 9–10
discipline, 140
discussants, 144
discussion section of papers, 103, 145
dissertations. *See* theses and dissertations
diversity, job search and, 120
Duke University, 42

The Edge (film), 21
edited volume, 144
electives, 41, 140
e-mail queries, 140
employment search. *See* job search
EndNote (online cite manager), 43, 54
ethnography, 65
exams: comprehensive exams (*See* comprehensive exams); qualifying exams (*See* qualifying exams)
Excel, 114
exhibit halls: at academic conferences, 88; defined, 144

Facebook, 36
faculty: assistant professors, 142; associate professors, 142; full professors, 142; graduate assistants, relationship with, 58–59; as mentors, 18–19; publishing and, 96; relationship with, 8; tenure (*See* tenure); transition to professorship (*See* professorship, transition to)
family considerations in job search, 123
Family Educational Rights and Privacy Act (FERPA), 140
financial management, 28–29
findings, 144
flexibility in job search, 123–24
Foss, Katherine A., 147–48
full professors, 142
full-time temps, 142

gender. *See* marginalized groups
gender identity. *See* marginalized groups
generational differences, 14
Getting What You Came For: The Smart Students Guide to Earning a Master's or PhD (Peters), 37
glossary, 139–45
goal setting, 5
Google Scholar, 109, 144
grading: graduate assistants, 60; teaching assistants, 56
grad-student rate, 144
graduate assistants, 49–61; anxiety, coping with, 57–58; authorship and, 60; balancing coursework, 49; communication in, 51–52; dangers of, 58–60; defined, 142; faculty, relationship with, 58–59; grading, 60; instructors of record, 50–51, 53, 143; overview, 10, 49–50; professional development, 53–54; recordkeeping, 60; reflection on, 61; research assistants (*See* research assistants); romantic relationships and, 59; stipends, 49–50; students, relationship with, 59–60; teaching assistants (*See* teaching assistants); tenure, considerations regarding, 54; time management in, 52–53; work procedures, 50–51
graduate directors, 142

graduate research assistants (GRAs), 56–57. *See also* research assistants
graduate student organizations, 21
graduate teaching assistants (GTAs), 55–56. *See also* teaching assistants
Graff, Gerald, 43
grants, importance of, 54
Greer, Jennifer, 11, 148
Gustafson, Bob, 84

Hannabach, Cathy, 32
Hardin, Marie, 11, 148
Harris, Carla, 27
Harris, Felicia, 26–27, 31
health insurance, 3
high-density sessions at academic conferences, 82–83, 145
hooks, bell, 31
Hopkins, Anthony, 21
housing, 2–3
human subject experiments, 47*n*11
hybrid courses, 140

"Identity Politics" (podcast), 32
"Imagine Otherwise" (podcast), 32
imposter syndrome, 57–58, 140
industry, 126–27
InsideHigherEd.com, 36
Inside Higher Education (journal), 114
Insight into Diversity (journal), 114
institutional review boards (IRBs), 38, 47*n*11, 144
instructors of record, 50–51, 53, 143
Interlibrary Loan (ILL) system, 20, 144
International Association for Media and Communication Research (IAMCR), 77
International Communication Association (ICA), 77, 82–83, 115
international students, 9, 17
interviews for jobs, 125
introduction section of papers, 144
Iowa State University, 73

Job Hub, 89
job search, 113–28; academic conferences and, 89; application letter, 121; "arms race" in, 121–22; attire for interviews, 125; beyond academic job market, 126–27; *curriculum vitae* and, 114–15, 117, 121; defining yourself in, 115; "demonstrated commitment," 119–20; diversity and, 120; family considerations in, 123; "fit" versus credentials, 125–26; flexibility in, 123–24; focus on during graduate school, 116–17; interviews, dos and don'ts, 125; location of, 115; mechanics of, 114–15; middle class employment, 117; networking and, 117–18; nonacademic careers, 126–27; organization in, 114; overview, 11, 113; practicing job talks and presentations, 124; "preferred" qualifications, 119; preparation for interviews, 125; publishing and, 101; references in, 122–23; "required" qualifications, 119; research and, 120; spreadsheets, 114; tailoring to position and location, 120–23; tenure and, 113, 117, 120, 123, 126; terminology of job advertisements, 119–20; theses and dissertations, impact of, 65, 118–19; vagaries of academic hiring, 115–16
Journal of Public Relations Research, 104
journals: guidelines, 106; selection of, 104–5; submission of papers to, 98–99, 104–6; transition to graduate school and, 15–16. *See also specific journal*

Keith, Susan, 10, 148
Kelsky, Karen, 29
keynote speaker, 144
Korean American Communication Association (KACA), 77

labs, 140
language barriers, 9
lectures, 141
letters of recommendation, 122–23

librarians, 19–20
Linder, Katie, 32
literature review, 66–67, 144
Lubbers, Chuck, 82

marginalized groups, 25–33; community connection and, 31–32; financial management, 28–29; mentors and, 27–28; micro-activism, 26; overview, 10, 25–26; overwork and, 26; personal dimension, 26–27; professional development, 29; professional dimension, 27–28; scholarly dimension, 29–30; self-care and, 26–27; stipends, 28–29; strategic outlook, 29–30; "weathering" and, 26
Master Class: Teaching Advice for Journalism and Mass Communication, 56
masters' theses, 43
maturity, 14
Mendeley (online cite manager), 43
mental health centers, 21
mentors: defined, 141; marginalized groups and, 27–28; professorship and, 130–31; transition to graduate school and, 18–19
Mergerson, Christoph, 43–44
method section of papers, 102–3, 144
micro-activism, 26
Microsoft Word, 114
minorities. *See* marginalized groups
moderators, 144
Modern Language Association, 106
MySpace, 36

National Center for Faculty Development and Diversity, 27
National Communication Association (NCA), 77, 83–84, 101, 115, 128n2
National Institutes of Health, 101
National Science Foundation, 100–101
networking: defined, 144; job search and, 117–18; professorship, transition to, 135–36
nonacademic careers, 126–27

office hours, 143
online cite managers, 43
online courses, 141
oral defense, 45, 63–64, 72–73
organizational politics, avoiding, 132–34
organizational sessions at academic conferences, 86–88
orientation, 141
other students: graduate assistants, relationship with, 59–60; relationship with generally, 8–9; theses and dissertations and, 71–72
out-of-convention sessions at academic conferences, 89

panel sessions, 145
papers: presentations at academic conferences (*See* presentations at academic conferences); publishing (*See* publishing)
parking, 3
path of study, selection of, 35–36
peer review process in publishing, 94–95, 145
Pennsylvania State University, 96, 101
Perlmutter, David D., 11, 148
Peters, Robert L., 37
podcasts, 32
popular articles, 145
posters at academic conferences, 83–85
PowerPoint, 83
Prather, Hugo, 13
preconferences, 145
pregnancy, 10
prelims, 6
preparation for graduate school, 3–6
prerequisites, 141
presentations at academic conferences, 79–86; actions to avoid, 84–85; authorship and, 85; feedback on, 86; formats of, 80; high-density sessions, 82–83; journals, submission to, 98–99; posters, 83–85; publishing (*See* publishing); traditional research papers, 80–81
presidents, 142

professional development: graduate assistants, 53–54; marginalized groups, 29; research assistants, 54; teaching assistants, 53

professorship, transition to, 129–37; advisors and, 130; brainstorming solutions, 136; getting noticed beyond immediate environment, 135; graduate students, relationship with, 133; mentors and, 130–31; minding your business, 132–34; networking and, 135–36; organizational politics, avoiding, 132–34; organizations and, 131; overview, 11, 129–30; path of study for, 36; professionalism and, 133; reputation, building, 134–35; self-confidence in, 137; tenure and, 132–33; work-life balance, finding, 136–37; writing and, 136. *See also* faculty

proposal meetings, 66–67

provosts, 142

Public Relations Inquiry, 104–5

Public Relations Review, 104

publishing, 93–111; abstract, 143; advisors and, 95–96; authorship in, 67; blind-review, 143; book chapter, 143; call for proposals (CFP), 143; collaboration in, 94, 96–97; conclusion section, 103–4, 145; coursework, balancing with, 98–99; critiques, responding to, 106–7; *curriculum vitae*, updating, 109–10; discussant, 144; discussion section, 103, 145; edited volumes, 144; expectations of, 99, 101; faculty and, 96; findings, 144; funding for, 100–101; guidelines of journals, 106; introduction section, 144; job search and, 101; journals, submission of papers to, 98–99, 104–6; knowledge area, building, 94; method section, 102–3, 144; other obligations, balancing with, 94; overview, 11, 93, 110–11; peer review process in, 94–95, 145; popular articles, 145; post-acceptance work, 109; preparation of manuscript, 105–6; purposes of, 93–95; quantity versus quality, 100; rejected manuscripts, 107–8; research for, 98; research project, setting up, 102; results, 144; reviewers, 105–8; revise and resubmit (R & R), 145; revisions, 106–7; sample, 144; selection of journals, 104–5; stages of, 101–10; structure of manuscript, 102–3; teams and, 96–97; tenure and, 94, 97–99, 104; theoretical framework, 144; thesis or dissertation topic and, 97–98; time frame for, 95

qualifying exams, 44–45; oral defense, 45; outcomes of, 45; preparing for, 44–45

R1 universities, 139

R2 universities, 139

race. *See* marginalized groups

reading: in coursework, 42–43; transition to graduate school and, 15–16

receptions at academic conferences, 88–89

references in job search, 122–23

RefWorks (online cite manager), 43, 54

religious organizations, 21

reputation, building, 134–35

research: job search and, 120; for publishing, 98; research agenda, 145; transition to graduate school and, 15

research assistants, 56–57; communication and, 51; defined, 142–43; overview, 50; professional development, 54; tips for, 57; work procedures, 51

"Research in Action" (podcast), 32

results, 144

reviewers, 105–8

revise and resubmit (R & R), 145

Rockquemore, Kerry Anne, 27, 29

romantic relationships, 59

Rosenberry, Jack, 83
Rutgers University, 41–42

Saleem, Ikhlas, 32
samples, 144
sample size, 65
scholarly writing, 145
scholar-to-scholar sessions at academic conferences, 83, 145
self-care, marginalized groups and, 26–27
self-confidence: professorship, transition to, 137; transition to graduate school and, 22
seminars, 141
sexual orientation. *See* marginalized groups
skipping class, 7
small liberal arts colleges (SLAC), 139
socials at academic conferences, 88–89
Stachowiak, Bonni, 32
stages of graduate school, 6–7
Stewart, James, 10, 149
stipends: defined, 141; graduate assistants, 49–50; marginalized groups, 28–29
stress, avoiding, 16, 43–44
student life offices, 21
student participation: in academic conferences, 78, 90–91; in class, 7–8, 14
study habits, 9
Sturgill, Amanda, 10, 149
"support staff," 19–20
syllabus, 7, 141

Taylor, Kevin P., 42
teaching assistants, 55–56; communication and, 51–52; defined, 142; grading, 56; logistical considerations, 55; notes, 56; overview, 50; professional development, 53; taking attendance, 56; textbooks, 56; tips for, 55–56; training, 56; work procedures, 51
"Teaching in Higher Ed" (podcast), 32

tenure: advisors and, 39–41; defined, 141; graduate assistants, considerations for, 54; job search and, 113, 117, 120, 123, 126; professorship, transition to, 132–33; publishing and, 94, 97–99, 104; tenure track, 142; theses and dissertations and, 64–65, 68–69
terminal degrees, 141
textbooks, 15, 56
theoretical framework, 144
theses and dissertations, 63–73; advisors and, 65, 71; "a-ha" moments and, 70; balancing rigor and manageability, 65; celebrating accomplishments, 72–73; challenges in writing, 68–70; committee members and, 65–66, 141; communicating progress, 71–72; data management, 70; defined, 143; delay, coping with, 67–68; developing proposal, 65–67; internal and external deadlines, 67; job search, impact on, 65, 118–19; literature review, 66–67, 144; masters' theses, 43; methodological alternatives, 65; narrowing scope of, 64–65; oral defense, 45, 63–64, 72–73; other students and, 71–72; overview, 10–11, 63–64; preliminary write-up, 66; pre-writing and pre-thinking, 68; proposal meetings, 66–67; proposals, 143; publishing and, 97–98; as stage of graduate school, 7; tenure and, 64–65, 68–69; theoretical framework, 144; time management, 66–68; "wilderness walk," 64; "writer's block," 68–69; writing accountability groups, 69; writing "heroes/heroines," 68
They Say, I Say: The Moves that Matter in Academic Writing (Graff and Birkenstein), 43
time management: defined, 141; graduate assistants, 52–53; theses and dissertations, 66–68; transition to graduate school and, 16–17

Tindall, Natalie, 27
traditional research sessions at academic conferences, 145
transition to graduate school, 13–23; adjustments in, 14; age differences and, 14; anxiety, coping with, 20–22; generational differences and, 14; mentors, 18–19; overview, 10, 13–14, 22–23; planning, 15–16; reading and, 15–16; research and, 15; schedule, establishing, 16; scouting campus, 17–18; self-confidence and, 22; "support staff," 19–20; time management, 16–17
transportation, 3
travel funding: academic conferences, 79–80; defined, 141; marginalized groups and, 29
Turabian style, 106
Twitter, 31, 36

underrepresented students. *See* marginalized groups
University of Alabama, 90
University of Kentucky, 90
University of North Carolina—Chapel Hill, 31, 42

vacations, 7–8, 45
Vafeiadis, Michail, 99
veterans' organizations, 21
visualization, 5–6

Walden, Ruth, 38
Waters, Richard D., 11, 149
"weathering," 26
Western Social Science Association (WSSA), 77
"wilderness walk," 64
work-life balance, finding, 136–37
writing: professorship, transition to, 136; publishing (*See* publishing); requirements, 42–43; theses and dissertations (*See* theses and dissertations); "writer's block," 68–69; writing accountability groups, 69; writing "heroes/heroines," 68

Zotero (online cite manager), 43, 54

www.ingramcontent.com/pod-product-compliance
Lightning Source LLC
Chambersburg PA
CBHW070642300426
44111CB00013B/2219